Born To Be Soldiers

Those Plucky Women of World War II

by

Kayleen Reusser

Kayleen Reusser Media

Born To Be Soldiers: Those Plucky Women of World War II first published in the United States by Kayleen Reusser Media. Printed in the United States.

Copyright © 2022 by Kayleen Reusser

KayleenReusser.com

ISBN: 979-8-9855897-0-2

Cover illustration by Kayleen Reusser. Printed in the United States of America

The information provided within this book is for general informational purposes only. While the author has tried to provide correct information, there are no representations or warranties, express or implied, about the completeness, accuracy, reliability, suitability or availability with respect to the information, products, services, or related graphics contained in this book for any purpose. Any use of this information is at one's own risk. Photographs are courtesy of individuals as named and the author.

Contents

Author's Note:

"It's a man's war."

"Women shouldn't be in uniform."

These statements and others were heard by the 350,000 American women who volunteered to serve their country in the military during World War II.

Each branch had its own identity, but their basic functions were similar -- that of freeing men for overseas assignments.

These were brave women who chose to serve their country against the wishes of family, friends and society.

The title 'born to be a soldier' comes from a statement made to me by Ruth Licking who served in the Army. It seemed incongruous at the time because she was 90 years old. Now I think otherwise.

Their indomitable spirit of these women remained with them throughout their lives and hopefully lives on through the re-telling of their stories in this book.

**

Thanks to Pam and Julie Sawusch, National WASP World War II Museum, Texas Woman's University, Marsha Ringenberg Wright for their help in putting this book together.

Foreword

While at a history fundraiser several years ago, I had the opportunity to meet Kayleen Reusser and discuss her books. I've been participating in living history events my entire life, portraying several eras but WWII WAC is by far my favorite. I got involved in WWII reenacting with my younger brother as a way to keep our grandfather's WWII service in our memories.

Through the research involved in creating this impression, I have become passionate about sharing the history and experiences of the women who served our country during the Second World War.

The courage and sacrifice of nearly 350,000 women who served in the US armed forces during WWII must be remembered —and being able to read stories through oral histories is crucial to keeping their memories alive.

I am so glad that Kayleen is making these women's stories more accessible through this volume so we can continue to recognize and honor their service.

-- Molly Sampson, Historian & Museum Professional

Women's Air Service Pilots (WASP)

Elizabeth 'Betty' White Dybbro

Elizabeth 'Betty' White was thrilled. A family member had offered to pay for her to ride in an airplane. In 1934 few people had even seen a plane. Betty knew none of her friends had ridden in one. The twelve-year-old couldn't wait to relay every detail.

The ride lasted less than an hour, but Betty loved every minute. From that day, she developed an intense interest in flying. Amelia Earhart, the famous American female aviator of the 1930s, became her hero.

After graduating from Ossian High School in Indiana in 1940, Betty studied at Manchester College. Deciding college was not for her, she quit after a year to work at General Electric in Fort Wayne.

When the war began in December 1941, that factory, like thousands around the country, began making parts for the war effort.

Betty wanted to serve her nation. But other than working in the factory and observing rationing, she didn't know what to do.

Since age 12, her interest in soaring through the skies had never waned. But there were no female pilots.

Then Betty read a magazine article about a new program in the military. Women were being recruited as pilots for the war effort. The article explained that female pilots would tow targets for anti-aircraft artillery practice, test planes, and ferry them to different bases. Their work would free men to serve overseas.

The women would be called Women's Air Service Pilots (WASP). Applicants were required to have 35 hours of flight time. Though it seemed impossible, as Betty, 19, had never taken a flight lesson, she knew this was the path for her.

From her salary at the factory, Betty paid for lessons at Smith Field in Fort Wayne. The cost of $10 per hour seemed exorbitant, but Betty saved money by not eating much.

After logging the required number of hours, Betty White drove to Sweetwater, Texas, where the WASP program was located. She wanted to see the program in action before applying.

Betty was impressed with the program and people at Sweetwater, especially Jacqueline Cochran, the founder and person in charge. The two got along well.

After attending a graduation ceremony for a WASP class, Betty was even more determined to be part of the program. She submitted her application on-site before returning to Indiana.

Her acceptance letter arrived a few weeks later. Betty was one of 25,000+ women who applied nationwide. Only 1,830 women were selected to train and serve as Army pilots.

Fearing her family would object to her decision, Betty left home for Texas in January 1944 without telling them. Her family learned about her decision in a newspaper article. They wrote to her, wishing her good luck.

The six-month WASP training program was equivalent to that given to male pilots. Ground school included college-level courses in math, physics, Morse code, and navigation. Morse code proved to be the hardest for Betty, but she eventually caught on.

In the afternoons the women, wearing belted men's jumpsuits because they had no official uniforms, completed hands-on training on the flight line with Stearman and AT-6 aircraft.

There were three phases of training -- primary, basic, advanced. During primary, Betty made the mistake of 'ground-looping'. Her plane had two wheels in the front. It was important upon landing to lock the rear wheel, the 'tail dragger.' If not locked, the plane would pull to the side. As in a car on ice, the pilot has to counteract the movement, while being careful not to overcorrect.

Unfortunately, Betty didn't lock the tail long enough and both wings of the plane were damaged. She was horrified, but her instructor did not deliver the serious reprimand which she expected. She never repeated that mistake.

One requirement for passing primary was being able to take an airplane engine apart and put it back together. At every stage of training the challenges increased.

In the basic phase the students learned how to navigate an aircraft by instruments only, should visibility during a flight be low. Before graduating, each women had to complete a 2,000-mile solo flight from Texas to California in an AT-6.

At any phase a student could 'wash-out' – fail to pass. Then she would be sent home, on her own expense, of course, as the WASP were not yet militarized.

In August 1944, Betty White had her wings pinned on her. She was one of only 1,102 women who would eventually complete the WASP program.

Not everyone was thrilled with women pilots. At her assigned base at Marfa, Texas, a male commander would not allow the WASPs fly. They were transferred to a gunnery school in Las Vegas, Nevada, where they towed targets with B-17's for live practice by male pilots. Some of the planes flown by WASPs were hit by erring shots. Thankfully, Betty's never was.

Another WASP task was to dive-bomb over gunners in the AT-6 to get range estimations.

They also flew the B-26, a big bomber used extensively throughout the European and Pacific Theaters.

By summer 1944, the war in Europe was winding down as Germany's resources were nearly expended. Male pilots, needing a rest from combat, were sent back to the States. With a sudden influx of experienced pilots, the Army decided the men could take over jobs being performed so ably by the WASP.

The announcement came that the WASP program would be disbanded on December 20, 1944. Betty and the other WASP were intensely disappointed, but there was nothing they could do. As Congress had never militarized the WASP, these same women had to pay their own way home.

The same was true for the families of the 38 women who had died in service to their country as WASP. The families had to pay for their daughters' bodies to be sent home. In many cases, other WASP donated money to help with the expenses of travel for the deceased.

Though she hated being out of the military, Betty was proud that she was one of the first women to fly American military aircraft. Together, she and the other WASP had flown almost every type of plane operated by the Army Air Corps during World War II, logging more than 60 million miles.

Betty had another bright spot in her life. She had met and fallen in love with a fighter pilot named Robert Sheehan. They married in 1945 and Betty lived with her in-laws in Washington State while her husband was sent to the Pacific to continue with the war there.

After the war ended, Betty and Robert became parents to two children. Sadly, Robert was recalled for the Korean War in the 1950s and was shot down. His body was never recovered.

Later, Betty married Phil Dybbro. Their family grew to include six children. The Dybbros lived in Fairbanks, Alaska, where they owned a store. Betty worked as a flight instructor for their business.

Decades went by when little mention was made of the women who had served their country so valiantly as military aviators.

Then, in 1977, the American military made a surprise announcement -- they would be training the first female military pilots.

The WASP and their families protested -- their women should be recognized as the nation's first female military pilots. The group lobbied in the nation's capital and their perseverance paid off. President Jimmy Carter granted the WASP status as veterans with full benefits.

Their recognition as World War II veterans continued on March 10, 2010, when each WASP (or members of her family if she was deceased or unable to make the visit) was presented with the Congressional Gold Medal in Washington DC.

Over the years, Betty White Dybbro has proudly spoken to groups about her military service and participated in WASP reunions.

In 2017, on her 95th birthday, members of a local flying club offered her the opportunity to fly in two planes, a Piper Cub and Stearman bi-plane -- the types of which she had flown as a young pilot. She accepted the offer and was accompanied by fellow pilots.

Despite more than 40 years passing since she had been in a cockpit, Betty said she felt 'comfortable and confident'.

Her thoughts: "Being a WASP was a wonderful experience. I really enjoyed it."

Elizabeth 'Betty' White Dybbro met Jackie Cochran, founder of the WASP program, before applying.

Margaret 'Maggie' Ray Ringenberg

She didn't look like a future pioneer.

Six-year-old Maggie Ray sat on her mother's lap, eyes riveted straight ahead. She was what some might call a tomboy, preferring to be outside on her family's farm near Hoagland, Indiana, than learning household tasks like baking pies.

Still, the youngest of three daughters born to Albert and Lottie Ray was unprepared for what awaited her that summer afternoon in 1927.

Maggie's family had been driving around their farm to look at crops when they spied a plane landing in a nearby field. Albert pulled the car over.

The pilot jumped out to greet them. He explained that he was a barnstormer, a sort of stunt pilot who performed tricks in the air for entertainment. When he asked the Rays if they would like to ride in the plane, the three girls clamored yes. Lottie shook her head. Her protests were overruled and the family hauled themselves aboard.

Maggie, perched on her mother's knees, loved the feeling of being aloft. But, unlike the rest of her family who looked over the sides of the plane for their farm far below, Maggie looked ahead, specifically between the seats. She wanted to see the dials of the plane to see how it worked.

The ride ended too soon for Maggie. The Ray family disembarked, and Albert paid the pilot before driving his family home. They talked along the way of their exciting adventure.

Although everyone (even Lottie) had enjoyed it, they could have no idea how that single event would plant a seed of interest in their youngest member. Indeed, Maggie would use it to re-think gender conventions of her day and decide for herself what a woman could – and should -- do with her life.

After graduating from Hoagland High School in 1940, Maggie considered her future. She had never forgotten her desire to be in a plane. As a fourth grader, her teacher had had to call her name several times when planes, rare as they were, flew past the school. Nothing could capture Maggie's attention or imagination like a plane.

But the only way Maggie knew to get in a plane was to be a stewardess. Pilots had to be men.

At that time, flight attendants were trained as nurses to help with possible ill health among passengers. Maggie decided to work at General Electric in Fort Wayne to pay for nursing school.

Then, one day, she had a thought -- what if the pilot became ill? Someone needed to know how to land. Maggie thought she should take flying lessons for this type of emergency.

When she told her father what she wanted to do, Albert Ray didn't respond. A week later, she repeated her desire to take flight lessons. Her father shocked her by saying he had researched area flight schools and recommended one to her.

With her father's blessing, Maggie began flight lessons. She soon lost interest in being a stewardess and focused on being a pilot.

Ground school classes were filled with men. It became obvious to everyone that the instructor didn't want Maggie in his class. He went out of his way to ask her the toughest questions. She was often embarrassed at not knowing the answers, but persevered because she wanted to learn. She didn't care what barriers lay ahead. She gave herself permission to fail and succeed.

Maggie took flight lessons from Pierce Flying Service -- only 30 minutes a week, because that was all she could afford. She also joined the newly-formed Civil Air Patrol (CAP).

Unlike her flight classes that were dominated by men, women were welcome in CAP. They were part of America's civilian aviation resources to aid the war effort on the home front.

As it happened, being a member of CAP was a huge advantage for Maggie as it put her at the right place at the right time.

In 1943, the Army Air Corps sent 21-year-old Maggie a telegram. It stated that she had the opportunity to be part of a new women's training detachment for the military. To apply she needed to go to the Palmer House in Chicago for an interview and exam.

Thrilled with the information, Maggie ignored the fact that she had recently had her appendix removed and needed time to heal. She purchased a train ticket to the Windy City. It would be her first ride on a train and her first trip to a major city.

Despite recent surgery and post-operative pain, Maggie passed her interview and physical, qualifying her for the WASP program.

In March Maggie left her home, but not before her family took a group photo. She wondered if her mother feared she would not return.

Supporting a daughter in the WASP was not the same for Albert and Lottie as if Maggie had joined the WAC or WAVES. The WASP was not militarized; therefore, Maggie's parents could not hang a blue star in their window signaling her military service.

If she would be killed, they would have to pay to have her body transported home.

When Maggie arrived at Sweetwater, Texas, she and the other 127 women in her class found an environment of intense heat, sand that made passing barrack inspections a challenge, and a wind that never ceased.

Their barracks contained six bays with six women in each. The six bays shared one latrine. Each of the women stowed her possessions in a small footlocker.

As they did not have uniforms, the women wore men's flight suits. The 'zoot suits' -- nicknamed for oversized men's suits popularized by jazz singers in the 1940s -- required the women to belt them and roll up the sleeves and pant legs.

The women learned to fly everything from trainers to large military aircraft, including the four-engine B-24 bomber.

Maggie Ray graduated in the fifth class of WASP on September 11, 1943. She was honored to have Jackie Cochran, founder and organizer of the WASP program, pin on her wings.

Of the 127 cadets who started the program six months earlier, 85 received wings. The others had 'washed out', due to being unable to pass the tests, suffering from ill health, or desire to leave the military.

Maggie was assigned to Air Transport Command, Second Ferrying Division, based at New Castle Army Air Base in Wilmington, Delaware. Her primary responsibilities were to pick up new planes, then test and fly them where needed. She was also assigned to fly decommissioned planes to boneyards (storage areas for aircraft retired from service).

Maggie became an excellent pilot. But she still encountered tricky, even life-threatening, assignments.

In 1943 she was flying a twin-engine transport from Bradley Field in Connecticut to a boneyard in Montgomery, Alabama. When she was over Washington, DC, the plane began to vibrate.

Maggie shut down each engine and restarted them to see if that was the problem. With no success she radioed the nearest tower and relayed her situation. She was told to ditch the plane and bail out over an unpopulated area.

Even though the plane was destined to be put out of use, Maggie hated to see it destroyed. Yet, as each minute passed and the vibration intensified, her chances of survival decreased.

Maggie believed she could maintain control of her plane and told the tower she could make the Army Air Force Base at Winston-Salem.

She managed to land safely, though as she shakily climbed out of the cockpit, evidence that her life had been in danger was evident -- raw gas leaked over the left engine.

The close encounter with death didn't diminish her thrill with flying. In spring 1944, Maggie was told her exceptional flying skills qualified her to be part of fighter training in P-47 Thunderbolts and P-51 Mustangs at Brownsville, Texas.

It was the first time American women had been allowed to fly the fighters equipped with guns which were being used in combat in Europe and the Pacific. Maggie reveled in the opportunity.

Unfortunately, the training was short-lived.

On her third day, Maggie and the other women were informed of the tragic news that two WASP pilots had touched wing tips, causing them to crash. Two students and an instructor died.

Maggie and many other of the women had known the deceased and grieved for them. They were then told another piece of news -- fighter training was disbanded until further notice. Each woman was given leave to return to her respective base.

Terribly disappointed and still trying to handle the news of the deaths of two of her sister pilots, Maggie returned to the Second Ferrying Division in Delaware where she resumed her regular duties.

A few months later, she received more bad news -- the WASP program was being deactivated in December 1944. Stateside jobs were needed for male pilots returning from the war.

On that final day, Maggie and the other WASP removed all military insignia from their uniforms. They paid for their transportation home.

Maggie left the WASP after passing check rides in a PT-19, BT-13, AT-6 and UC-78. She earned her instrument rating in a DC-3 and co-piloted a C-54.

At home in Indiana Maggie Ray put away her uniforms in the back of her closet. But, although she looked as though she had pushed aside her interest in flying, she had not.

The former WASP enlisted in the Reserves, earning the rank of First Lieutenant. She would be discharged in 1947.

In March 1945 Maggie earned her instructor rating and worked for Pierce Flying Service, the business from which she had taken lessons before the war. She gave private lessons and flew for area businesses.

In August, Maggie was again part of the war effort when officials at a local radio station hired her to fly over Fort Wayne, dropping leaflets announcing Japan's surrender. Fort Wayne's newspapers were on strike, just at the time when a surrender by the Japanese was imminent. She was thrilled to do so.

In 1946, Maggie's life seemed to settle on the ground as she married Major Morris Ringenberg of the Army Corps of Engineers. They lived near Fort Wayne and became parents to two children.

But Margaret, as she now preferred to be called, was far from being done with flying. She balanced Girl Scout meetings and cooking Sunday meals after church with competing in round-the-world air races. She would, in fact, compete well into her 70's.

In 2001, Margaret Ringenberg attracted national attention when television newscaster Tom Brokaw featured her in a chapter of his New York Times best-selling book, *The Greatest Generation*.

In 2007 she was picked during the Gathering of Eagles at Maxwell Air Force Base in Alabama as one of 16 pilots who had attained recognition in the field of aviation.

The following year Margaret was inducted into the International Women in Aviation Pioneer Hall of Fame at the Women in Aviation International Conference in San Diego.

Margaret became a member of The Ninety Nines, Experimental Aircraft Association, Air Race Classic Association, Smith Field Association, and speaker for NASA Distinguished Lecture Series.

One of her favorite annual events to attend was the Experimental Aircraft Show in Osh Kosh, Wisconsin. Each year the WASP met to chat and renew their camaraderie.

In July 2008, Margaret drove alone from her home in Indiana to Osh Kosh. On the morning of July 28, 2008, she was found in bed, having died in her sleep.

During her lifetime, Margaret Ray Ringenberg logged more than 40,000 flight hours in hundreds of aircraft.

The pioneer, who as a six-year-old dreamed of flying a plane, had seen her dreams come true.

Her thoughts:

"My dad, Albert Ray, always said there was nothing too hard for me to accomplish. He believed I could do anything I put my mind to, including becoming a pilot. I proved him right."

Military note:

When the WASP community needed a female flying mascot to represent their unique women, it turned to Walt Disney. He created a female gremlin based on the book, *The Gremlins*, written by British author Roald Dahl.

According to British military aviation folklore, a gremlin was a mischievous source of any unknown problem. Disney's drawing of a WASP gremlin was a small female winged figure coming in for a landing sporting horns, yellow flight cap, red top, yellow slacks, long black gloves, red high-top boots, and goggles. Fifinella, as the WASP gremlin was named, was sewn as patches to the women's flight jackets.

Margaret 'Maggie' Ray Ringenberg flew more than 40,000 miles in dozens of aircraft throughout her lifetime.

Mary Anna 'Marty' Martin Wyall

She thought it was a cross between girl scout camp and jail.

Mary Anna Martin 'Marty' Wyall made this statement during an interview decades after completing WASP training in Sweetwater, Texas. Truth was, she loved every minute of it.

Her enthusiasm was obvious in the dozens of letters she wrote home during that time.

Mary Anna Martin was born on January 24, 1922, in Liberty, Indiana. Her father, Sumner Martin, was a Methodist minister, meaning the Martin family moved often as he was assigned to different churches. Mary Anna's mother, Bernice Martin, cared for the couple's four children.

In 1939, Mary Anna graduated from Shields High School in Seymour, Indiana, before enrolling at MacMurray's Women's College in Jacksonville, Illinois, on a music scholarship. Deciding music was not for her, she transferred to DePauw University near Greencastle, Indiana, to major in bacteriology.

During her sophomore year, Mary Anna was moved to tears at hearing about the terrible events at Pearl Harbor on December 7, 1941, and the deaths of 2,403 men and injuries to hundreds of others.

Mary Anna vowed to help her country; she just didn't know how.

Then she read a magazine article about a new program with the Army – one that was recruiting women to fly military aircraft.

Mary Anna was intrigued with the idea. She wanted to apply to the WASP program, but her father insisted that she graduate from college first. Mary Anna reluctantly obeyed.

After graduating from DePauw, Mary Anna worked at Eli Lilly, a pharmaceutical firm. She saved money from her earnings to pay for 35 flight hours required of applicants at Sky Harbor in Indianapolis.

After completing the WASP paperwork, Mary Anna was thrilled to be informed she had been chosen from among the 25,000 applicants to become a member of the WASP.

Not everyone wanted Mary Anna to join the WASP. Bernice Martin thought it was wrong for a woman to be in the military. She refused to say good-bye to her daughter on the day of Mary Anna's departure.

Mary Anna understood her mother had been born and raised in an era in which women didn't work outside of the home. Mary Anna told her mother she would have to accept the decision.

Sumner hugged his daughter good-bye. He expressed his pride in her efforts. Eventually, Bernice would change her mind about Mary Anna's decision.

There was yet another obstacle before Mary Anna could fly. On Easter Day 1944 she left by train for Sweetwater, Texas. She was just getting ready to reboard the train in Oklahoma following a quick stop when she received a telegram from her parents – Mary Anna's WASP papers were not in order. She needed to go home.

Confused, Mary Anna returned to Indiana to discover the form for her medical exam was missing from her application. When she contacted the flight surgeon who had given her the exam to ask about the form, he replied, "It's on my desk."

Baffled, Mary Anna asked why he had not submitted it. He said, "I don't think women should be in the military."

Mary Anna controlled her temper long enough to say, "I don't think anyone has the right to tell me I can't do something before I even try."

She said a few more things before the doctor, who had served in the military, interrupted. "Young lady, that is no way to talk to an officer." In the end he sent in the form and Mary Anna was re-assigned to the next class of WASP.

On May 26, 1944, she arrived at Avenger Air Field for training with class 44-W-10.

During the next six months, Mary Anna, who was nicknamed 'Marty', never seemed to tire of the rigors of flight training.

When the program closed in December 1944, she was classified as a member of the last class of WASP. After the war, she continued flying and took an active part in WASP reunions and activities. She served as the WASP historian for decades.

Before her death in 2017, Marty donated her materials to Texas Women's University for its WASP collection.

The following are excerpts from her letters in that collection. They give a personal view of what one young woman experienced as her life was forever changed as a WASP.

**

Tuesday, June 13

W-10 is really getting into the spirit of Avenger. Tonight there was really a free for all trying to duck everyone who soloed PT's today. Saturday the 1st girl soloed and perhaps by end of the week we will have all soloed. Three of my bay-mates swam with the fishes in the wishing well.

This was my first really bad day. I knew I had a chance to solo, so I tried too hard. However, tomorrow I'm going to fly with a different attitude.

This morning we had quite a lengthy lecture on techniques of using a parachute. One of the officers had been in a special school for parachute instructors and we are to get quite a lot of training in the future!

The ironic thing of all is that this evening at supper I heard that a girl was killed this morning in an AT6 because she jumped too close to the ground... she evidently tried to ride the ship in and decided too late to jump. We were just told today that if there's any doubt at all that the ship is going to crash – Jump! Noble pilots are not always safe pilots.

We got our dog tag yesterday and I feel like a honest-to-goodness wasp now. On the tag it says "Mary A. Martin WASP" ...

Mother you asked about the shots. The more we get shot the less the reaction is. It's really not bad at all. You walk in one door and while you pass down the hall to the other door you feel a slight prick. That's all! This Saturday we get our 2nd tetanus shot, wait 3 more weeks for our last one. That, we hope, is the last one for another year.

Boy, the sand here is getting to be quite a problem. I wash out a shirt almost everyday, the water is a muddy color. I hang it up to dry and the shirt acquires a muddy color. Nevertheless I iron it, and consequently the shirt as well as everything is getting a sandy color.

**

Thursday June 15

Happy Dad's Day! I've got some good news for you. I hope it will compensate for flowers or somepin. I <u>soloed</u> yesterday. It was a wonderful feeling and made Mr. Bingham quite happy. We have been really hep on flying this week. The instructors are all anxious to get his students soloed. It's a grand old feeling to be up there all alone.

The most thrilling thing just happened a few minutes ago. Three B-17's (Flying Fortresses) buzzed the field in formation and then peeled off to land one at a time. A jeep rushed out to the planes and took the pilots to the O.D. (Officer of the Day) office.

By that time everyone had rushed to the flight line to get the deal. Guess why they came. To pick up the girls from W-5 for a dance tonight. The girls in the graduate class were guests of honor. Wouldn't that be wonderful to go to a dance about 100 m away in a B-17. I hope that happen to W-10 around in December.

I'll let you in on a little military secret. Miss Cochran was here this week. She ate in the dining room with W-10 this noon. She's very charming and make you at home.

**

June 22

This has really been a drooling week. Things are popping thick and fast. We have finals in Math and Theory of Flight tomorrow which will finish up those courses. Next week we start maps and charts and physics.

I now have 19 hours flying time (5 hrs. 20 min. solo). I had a civilian progress check ride last Tuesday and messed it up. So I have to take another one soon. Perhaps tomorrow! Then my 20 hrs. Army check will be Saturday, I think.

The W-10's are washing out right and left. Most have been resignations (can't take Army life) -- some have been medical discharges and of course some have not been able to fly good enough.

**

Thursday, June 30th

Dearest Everybody,

Gee, this has been an exciting week. First I must tell you I passed my civilian recheck Friday and passed my 20 hour Army check Monday morning. It really made me happy.

Today I have over 30 hours (11 solo) and am starting on the acrobatic stage. That's about all we do from now on in P. T's. The more I do them the better I like acrobatics. At first it scared me silly to do a spin, but after doing some everyday for a couple of weeks I've lost my tenseness. I actually can count the turns now.

Tuesday, the 27th, was graduation here at the field. It was the most impressive thing I've witnessed. It was 100 times more thrilling than college graduations. A band from Barkeley played for us. The classes all sat in the center section of the gym.

After we had all filed in the graduating class in their blue uniforms marched in and we stood to sing the Army Air Corps song. The commanding officer gave about a one-minute speech and the wings were presented to the W-5 girls. Then as a tradition each class sings an original farewell song to the graduates.

Tomorrow was the day for the new class to come but Gen. Arnold made the announcement Tuesday (as you must know) that no more WASP training classes would enter. Whew! -- I'm glad I'm here!

The officials have definitely assured us that we will graduate. This has become quite an exclusive program.

There are about 30 girls here that were expecting to enter the June class. I feel so sorry for them. They all are just heart-sick -- especially after seeing Avenger Field. They looked like a good bunch of kids too. Just think we will never be upper classmen -- always the babies.

**

July 17

Last night after taps we had a visitor ship come in -- forced landing. It was before bedcheck and we heard this plane circling the field. There were no lights on [the] field which made it rather difficult for them to land. In fact,

And everyone filed out of bed to go to the flight line. Strict Army discipline didn't have much control then. It was really very funny and the two Army officers who landed looked the situation over and said "We've never had a reception quite like this before." They weren't expecting to see gals, anyway.

**

July 24, 1944

Dearest Folks, Wow, what a life -- I passed all my check rides for primary. I have about 60 hours and have been having lots of fun in the last few days practicing acrobatics. Today Cappy (a baymate of mine) and I had a rendezvous at the far end of our practice area and watched each other do loops, snap rolls, vertical reverse, slow rolls and inverted flight. It was really sport!

**

August 4

I have finished 1/3 of my training and am about to start on AT- 6's. It has a horsepower of 650 and the cockpit at this point looks like a big mechanical monster with 26 faces glaring at me and daring me try and fly it (which I can't). However, in the next 3 weeks I should be able to solo.

**

August 15

I am about to solo the AT-6. Probably this week sometime or maybe next Monday. ... I'm sure we'll solo soon. The ground school classes are quite interesting now. We have 3 hrs. a day.

**

August 24

I wish somehow you could see the operation here. I have never had a feeling of regret. I just look around and say to myself, "Gee, all this is for me!" (Tomorrow I get fitted for our blue uniforms. So we'll be sure and have them for Christmas I suppose.) Another morale booster.

**

Sept 2

Today was really a killer. I flew both afternoon and morning besides an hour in the link trainer and a 2-hour lecture about flying the civil airways in instrument weather. My total flight time was 4 hours including a civilian check ride (which was a push-over).

**

September 12, 1944

Dearest Folks, Whew! What a schedule. Each phase I think "well, if I get thru this it will be smooth sailing." However, they each get worse. This time it's rushing around all day besides so much studying and concentration we have to do for ground school and flying.

Today I flew the BT-13. It's a better ship than I expected. From what the upper classmen said I thought it would be like flying a tub after the AT-6.

**

September 25

Well, Dad, you may have been gassed in World War I, but I was gassed in this one. When I tell my grandchildren about it just watch their eyes bug out. Last week we had about 6 hours of lectures about war gasses in this war -- their effectiveness and uses. On the last day we had a factual demonstration out on the drill field.

Our instructor set off charges of the various gasses and we ran thru these to get a whiff of their characteristic odors. We had mustard, Lewisite, chloropicrin and phosgene. The phosgene was the most dangerous and we had one casualty.

One girl over did it a bit and inhaled too much of the choking gas and almost chocked to death. She was in the hospital 2 days. We all had watery eyes from the demonstration and the odors stayed on our clothes.

**

October 8, 1944

Last Tuesday evening we heard an announcement over the radio that the WASP program would be closed Dec. 20. It was quite a shock for all of us. All this training without a chance to use it. Then Mrs. Deaton called a meeting for all WASPs and trainees on the field.

She gave us the news officially. But then told us something that made us cheerful too. C.A.A. has verbally promised to give all graduate WASPs a commercial license. That means I can take anyone up for a ride and can charge them for it, and it also means I can work towards my instructor's rating which is pretty hard to get.

We get to keep our uniforms after the 20th of Dec. Oh yes, our graduation date has been set for the 9th of December.

**

October 17, 1944

Dearest Folks, We had a very tragic thing happen this morning. One of the girls in 44-W-9 crashed on the long 2,000 mile cross country. It hit some of the girls in her class pretty hard. It seems that we go along so long that accidents never enter our minds.

The news of her death so shocked the entire field that our e. 0. and one of the staff officers immediately flew over to Memphis, Tenn. to take care of the situation. And they are trying to keep it as secret as possible so that it will not get into the newspapers. We haven't the slightest idea what happened, except that she was off-course and was evidently lost.

However, we have had a marvelous record when it comes to fatal accidents, in fact, it is very much higher than the cadet record. But don't you worry about me. I'll always get her down sunny-side-up somehow.

**

14, November 1944

Dearest Mother and Dad, Last night, I went on a short cross country from 8:00 to 10:00. The lights were beautiful, so early in the evening all the farmers were still up and we could see little lights lit up all over the country. About 100 miles east of us we saw a thunderstorm from the lightning it ejected.

Down here they never ask you IF you can do it, rather they say "You've shown me you can do it, now go up and prove it to yourself." It certainly must take men of faith to be instructors.

My trip last week was truly the thrill of the lifetime. We started Wednesday morning about 10:00 and flew into Avenger about 1:00 Sunday afternoon.

The whole trip took in eight states, and we flew over some beautiful spots. The trip from Ft. Sumner to Pueblo was the most wonderful experience since I have started flying. It was through the mountains, and with the clouds and snow around the peaks it made quite a picture. I had to fly at about 12,000 feet most of the way to clear the tops enough to avoid the downdrafts. Some peaks on my left quite a distance were from 14,000 to 16,000 feet high.

**

November 28, 1944

Dearest Mother and Dad,

I'm just about finished with all my flying time. Have only a couple hours of formation and perhaps an hour of acrobatics. Sunday afternoon the rest of us who haven't been down to San Antonio for the pressure tests are going down.

I certainly wish one of you could come down. This graduation means more to me than any college degree could ever mean..

**

December 7

Dearest Folks, Well the big day is over and I'm really excited! Those wings are certainly beautiful. The graduation affair was really one for the books.

Gen. Arnold presented the wings and Miss Cochran gave us our diploma.

Well, I must go now -- I was just invited to play pool with a nice lieutenant. Love, Mary Anna

**

Military note:

During the final WASP graduation of which Marty was part, General Hap Arnold, Commanding General of the Army Air Force, told the class: "You and more than 900 of your sisters have shown that you can fly wingtip to wingtip with your brothers. If ever there was any doubt in anyone's mind that women can become skillful pilots, the WASP have dispelled that doubt. I want to stress how valuable I believe the whole WASP program has been for the country. We of the Army Air Force are proud of you, we will never forget our debt to you."

&&

Although 1,074 WASP graduated at Sweetwater, there were actually 1,102 WASP. Prior to the war, Nancy Harkness Love trained 28 pilots for what was called the Women's Auxiliary Ferrying Squadron (WAFS). The two groups were joined in 1943 for the WASP program and Love became the Executive under Jackie Cochran.

.

Mary Anna Martin 'Marty' Wyall served as a WASP historian for decades after the war.

Women's Army Corps (WAC)

Frances Kraner Beeler – Army Nurse Cadet

As a young woman, Frances Kraner desired a career as a nurse. The problem was, she had no way of working towards that goal.

Frances had been born in 1923 on a farm in Adams County, Indiana. Her parents, Russell and Gladys Kraner, struggled like many other Americans during the 1930s, to provide for Frances and her sister, Elmira.

Frances liked living in her small town and attending church with friends. However, she dreamed of something more for her life.

While growing up, Frances' family often cared for sick relatives. Although no one in her family was a nurse, Frances learned how to care for sick people and felt called to the nursing profession.

But her family didn't have money for nursing school. So, after graduating from Geneva High School in 1941, Frances worked in a restaurant.

After war was declared in December, she found a job at General Electric in Decatur, Indiana, making parts for the war effort.

Then, in early 1942, Frances heard about a new program from the Army that seemed to be the answer to her prayers. An Army recruiter told her that nurses and doctors were desperately needed for the war effort. The Army would pay for a woman's education to become a nurse if she would commit to a certain amount of time in service afterward.

Frances believed enlisting in the Army was her way to becoming a nurse. A woman had to be 21 years old to enlist. The only way around this was with written permission from a parent or guardian.

When 20-year-old Frances told her parents what she wanted to do, they agreed that Frances should have the chance to pursue her love of nursing. They signed the paperwork providing consent.

Frances had another reason for wanting to serve her country. She had been engaged to a young soldier who was killed while fighting in Italy. She grieved for him and was resolved to do what she could to help America win the war.

Following basic training, Frances was sent to work at Fitzsimmons General Hospital in Denver. She realized right away that the recruiter had not been kidding; there was an intense need for medical staff.

Frances and other nursing students attended classes in the mornings. Afternoons were dedicated to hands-on training with soldiers who had returned to the United States for intensive medical care. The young men had incurred some of the worst injuries imaginable from fighting around the world.

After being injured, they would have first been treated at field hospitals on battlefields. If further care was needed, the soldiers were shipped to England and then, in case of amputations or serious illness, sent back to the United States to receive even more comprehensive treatment.

There were a number of wards at Fitzsimmons, including psychiatric, diabetic, and venereal. The wards were made up of long rooms with approximately 16 beds in each.

Army Surgical Technician Frances Kraner learned to give shots and bandage wounds. She worked with patients of tracheotomies and assisted in their cleaning.

When she didn't faint during autopsies, she was assigned to surgeries. In the ear, nose, and throat clinic, she assisted in removing tonsils.

She and the other nurses worked on holidays and during special events.

After a transfer to Beaumont General Hospital at Beaumont, Texas, Frances adapted to treating limbs with frostbite on soldiers who had fought outdoors in winter. Sometimes the loss of circulation to their extremities caused gangrene had set in. The stench of the infection filled the room and Frances tried not to show her repugnance while treating the patients with a smile.

When redressing a patient's foot where the infection was rampant, a toe would fly off. Frances calmly proceeded with the bandaging as though nothing had happened.

She learned about new drugs and was especially enthralled with penicillin. The drug's effectiveness at slowing the rate of infection thrilled her.

The only problem Frances encountered was in giving shots. She thought the needles were huge!

Once, when she was giving a soldier a shot, the needle broke in his arm. Frances was mortified. A doctor used forceps to retrieve it, all the while gently teasing her about it.

The needles were cleaned after each use as supplies were limited. Hardly anything was thrown away.

On Sundays, medical staff assisted patients to chapel services in the hospital. Their name for the line was 'Tuners Trolley.'

Frances became fond of her medical staff and patients. On her 22nd birthday she took a bouquet of roses sent to her from friends and distributed them to patients. They, in turn, sang to her. Frances very much enjoyed the camaraderie.

Even when she was off-duty, Frances wrote letters for soldiers. The letters were written on Vmail to save costs, plus it was free to military personnel.

The hospital also treated German soldiers who had been wounded and taken prisoner during the war. They were sent to America for their imprisonment and guarded on the wards by military police.

To Frances, they appeared to be young – maybe 14 years old. As the Germans healed, they were assigned simple jobs in the hospital, such as mopping floors. They seemed happy to work there.

Still, as Frances spied them in the halls, she tried not to think of the fiancé she had lost. She knew others on the hospital staff felt the same begrudging acceptance, especially as this new work force helped keep the hospital running.

Private Frances Kraner remained at Beaumont Hospital until December 1945 when she was discharged. She boarded a troop train for the long trek home. Male soldiers filled the seats and aisles; no civilians were allowed to allow more soldiers to get home.

Despite her experiences of helping injured men during the past year and a half, Frances felt shy and awkward on the train. Surrounded by so many young men, she pulled out her crochet project and kept her head bent as she worked the stitching. She needn't have worried. The soldiers ignored her as the train headed north.

The trip seemed interminable to Frances who thought the conductor stopped at every telephone pole! She was anxious to see her family, but Frances had another reason to hurry home -- she had a wedding to plan.

Corwin Beeler was a childhood friend who had spent four years as a plane mechanic at a South American air base. Early in the war, Corwin had been engaged to another woman. When she sent him a 'Dear John' letter in a desire to break off their relationship, he had been disappointed but free to date other women.

When Frances and Corwin had been home at the same time during their leaves, they renewed their friendship. They roller skated, fished, and sang in church. When Frances and Corwin left for their mutual bases, they promised to write letters. Gradually, the friendship deepened into a romance. By the time the war was over, they were engaged.

They married in Geneva on December 31, 1945.

The pair became parents to five children. Corwin worked as a truck driver for General Electric in Decatur. Frances worked in nursing at a local retirement community.

Her thoughts: "I was always glad to have the opportunity to serve my country as a nurse. I may not have helped to win the war, but I helped."

Frances Kraner Beeler signed up with the Army to learn nursing skills that helped her find employment throughout her life.

Charlotte Koch Eisenhart -- WAC

When Japanese forces bombed Pearl Harbor on December 7, 1941, the following day the American Congress declared war on Japan, Italy, and Germany -- the Axis nations.

Charlotte Koch of Urbana, Indiana, wanted to help her country at war. What surprised the 23-year-old was that her choice of duty in serving meant she had to fight her own countrymen as well.

Charlotte Koch was born in 1918 to William and Charlotte Koch. After graduating from Urbana High School in 1936, she worked at a number of jobs, including sales clerk at Wolf & Dessauer Department Store and manager of Meyers Brothers Drug Company, both located in Fort Wayne, Indiana.

Two years had passed since the war began. Charlotte never forgot about her desire to help her country. She and her family did what they could to observe rationing of food and other goods, all for the purpose of providing sufficient materials for soldiers. But Charlotte wanted to do more.

In August 1943, Charlotte heard about an Army program that might make that longing possible.

The Women's Army Auxiliary Corps (WAACs) had formed in 1942 to allow women to take over jobs previously held by men. These ranged from baking, clerical, driving and medical. Later, the WAACs were assigned a larger variety of tasks as their capabilities were recognized.

The women's presence enabled the men to be relieved to go overseas to battle.

Charlotte thought the program sounded ideal for her. Her parents, unlike those of many young women who wanted to serve in the military, were supportive of her decision. They teased, saying they hoped the Army could teach her to take orders better than they could.

Charlotte was not the only member of her family to join the WAACs. Younger sister Ethel Marie, known as 'Snooks' by her family, also signed up. She would serve in the South Pacific and the two sisters would write many letters to each other.

Charlotte's two other sisters, Alice and Rosaleen, helped make jeeps at International Harvester in Fort Wayne. Their efforts would be recognized decades later as 'Rosie the Riveters.' The two Koch sons, Lawrence and Paul, were deferred for farming.

Charlotte began her military service with six weeks of basic training at Fort Oglethorpe, Georgia, located 90 minutes north of Atlanta. While there, she received letters from friends and family who conveyed something of concern -- strangers were in her tiny hometown asking questions about Charlotte.

And not just any strangers were asking the questions – it was the FBI!

Charlotte was shaken at the thought of why the FBI would be looking into her life. She had never been accused of a crime. But she had little time to think about the matter as, after basic training was completed, she and other WAACs were sent to a college in Conway, Arkansas, to learn basic office skills for future assignments.

At the WAAC school, Charlotte completed a six-week course in policies and procedures of administration, while receiving specific training in military correspondence, record keeping, and reports.

She was already experienced with meticulous work practices from her other jobs. At Meyers Brothers Charlotte had approved the menu for the shop's soda fountain, ordered supplies, interviewed job applicants, checked cash registers, made daily reports to the manager, monitored employee time records, and acted as hostess. Basically, anything the manager needed done to help in the running of the store, Charlotte had been trusted to perform.

Upon graduation, Charlotte traveled by train with other WAACs to Seattle's Port of Embarkation. It was a busy, bustling place. Troops boarded ships headed for the Pacific or returned through there.

Charlotte was assigned as receptionist in an office on the base. Her efficient manner enabled her to help set up the mail facility, file receipts, type letters, prepare monthly work load reports, and supervise four enlisted women and one enlisted man. She worked from 0800 to 1700 hours (8:00am-5:00pm), five days a week.

She and the other WAACs observed military dress code with uniforms of khaki-colored jackets, ties, skirts, and shirts. On their feet they wore brown oxfords. Their hair had to be above the collar, either cut short or pinned. On non-working days they could wear a seersucker military dress but never pants.

The women were billeted at local hotels; Charlotte was assigned to the Stratford. Each room contained two Army cots -- no beds. The WAAC program was so new that the women assembled their own cots. The mess hall (dining room) was in the basement of the hotel.

At the end of each work day, the women were picked up by an Army driver and returned to their hotels. The rest of the evening was theirs for writing letters, playing cards, reading or visiting.

The standard pay for a WAAC was $21 per month. Because the Army provided her food and clothing, Charlotte didn't need much money and sent funds from her paycheck to her family.

After several weeks in Seattle, Charlotte finally discovered why the FBI had been asking questions about her. She had been investigated to ensure suitability for a position of responsibility in Seattle.

Eventually, Charlotte was assigned as secretary to a general. She knew everything at her work was important and confidential. She was careful not to talk about it outside of the office.

Her duties included handling classified mail. At one point she read the words 'Manhattan Project' stamped on papers that came across her desk.

At that time Charlotte – like most Americans -- didn't know what the term meant. But in August 1945, nearly everyone around the world would know of the scientific program in Los Alamos, New Mexico, organized to create a bomb that would eventually help to win the war.

Handling classified documents was not the only challenge to Charlotte's job. By volunteering to serve their country in the military, she and other WAACs encountered antagonism by people -- male soldiers and civilians – who didn't approve of women wearing military uniforms or calling themselves soldiers.

Charlotte and the other women learned to live with those attitudes. Gradually, the public's opinions improved as the women proved themselves honorable and capable of handling jobs assigned to them.

The only other detriment to being in the Army in Seattle, in Charlotte's opinion, was the weather – it seemed to rain from October through May.

On August 31, 1943, a major change occurred for the WAACs when the program was disbanded. Those women who had volunteered to serve in the Army were dismissed and told to go home.

After absorbing the shock, however, the women learned that was not the entire story. The following day a new branch – the Women's Army Corps (WAC) -- was formed. This was an official arm of the military with female members given full military benefits. Any WAAC who wanted to re-enlist as a WAC was urged to do so.

Charlotte Koch was one of more than 45,000 WAACs who re-enlisted. Her duties and uniforms remained what they had been before the change.

In December 1944, the WACs at Seattle were given a special request – would they decorate their mess hall and visit with soldiers who would arrive there for a party? The goal was to help the young troops manage the Christmas season.

The answer was a resounding YES!

Many of the men traveling through Seattle were new recruits away from home for the first time. Dining with the WACs in their hotel mess hall under festive decorations, the men – some just 17 years old -- relaxed enough to admit their fears of combat. The WACs listened and chatted, doing what they could to ease the men's trepidation of heading overseas.

Soldiers returning from the Pacific presented more of a challenge. They didn't want to talk about the war. Later, after hearing stories about the battles on various islands, the women understood their reticence.

Charlotte Koch enjoyed military life. She had made friends with people around the nation, held a position of trust, and was paid a decent salary.

She especially enjoyed getting to know an Army soldier named Russell Eisenhart.

Russ, as he preferred to be called, drove the bus that transported the WACs to and from work each day. As he and Charlotte chatted, she learned he was from Pennsylvania. They spent much off-duty time together.

A few months later in a letter Charlotte wrote to her sister Alice, she penned thoughts about the relationship (date unknown):

"Alice, I sure wish you were here so I could talk to you. Yes, about a man. This is strictly confidential and please don't say anything to the folks. I think I told you about Russ that I've been dating for two months and have known for a year.

Since I've gone out with him, I've found he is a lot different than I thought he was. I like him very much and we always have a good time when we go out. He is very serious, wants to marry me when we get out of the Army. Everything is so uncertain. He doesn't know what he wants to do except he doesn't want to go back home which is Penn. Yes, he's a Penn. Dutchman. He's a couple years younger than I am but says, what's the difference. Says, I will look as sweet when I'm 70 to him as I do today. Isn't that sweet?

I can't quite seem to make up my mind. He would certainly be good to me cause he really thinks a lot of me; has for the last year, as everyone at the port knows...

I won't do anything rash. Love, Charlotte.

By the time the war ended with the Japanese surrender at Tokyo Harbor in September 1945, Staff Sergeant Charlotte Koch had made up her mind. Russ Eisenhart had proposed marriage and she accepted. Charlotte couldn't wait to go home to plan their wedding.

Charlotte was not discharged until January 1946.

Russell Eisenhart was discharged in February 1946. He and Charlotte were married in April. They lived in Chicago for two years where Russ worked as a truck mechanic. They moved to Fort Wayne to be near Charlotte's family and became parents to one son.

Her thoughts: "Military life was a challenge. But I enjoyed it and meeting people from around the country. The war united us as a nation. The entire country fought and endured sacrifices. We all worked to make sure we'd win."

Charlotte Koch Eisenhart helped set up the WAC barracks in Seattle Port of Embarkation.

Ruth Cooper Licking -- WAC

The bombing of Pearl Harbor in 1941 inspired men to leave their jobs and head to battles overseas. By 1942, the government was issuing contracts to factory owners across the country to convert facilities to munitions plants. Cities like Detroit were building planes, military vehicles, and more.

When several of Ruth Cooper's friends from her hometown of Marion, North Carolina, left to work in Detroit, she wanted to do the same.

But her parents, especially her mother, objected to Ruth leaving home. Detroit was too big of a city and it was too far away.

Ruth had been born in 1921. Part of her teaching while growing up was to obey her parents. The Depression of the 1930s meant the Coopers with their eight children (Ruth had five sisters and two brothers) had had to work together to save money, from caring for their big garden to wearing hand-me-down clothing.

After graduating from Marion High School in 1938, Ruth worked at Belk-Broome Department Store in Marion for three years.

She had a job. And yet, with the start of the war, something had changed for her.

Ruth was 22 years old. Some of her friends were married and had children. She believed she was old enough to decide where to work.

But Ruth didn't head to Detroit to work in a factory. Instead, she joined the Women's Army Auxiliary Corps (WAACs).

No one in Ruth's family was in the military. She was breaking new ground.

Rather than feel terrified at the way her life might change, Ruth was thrilled. She attended church and believed God intended her to be a soldier.

First, she had to pass the physical examination.

After receiving a day off of work, Ruth traveled by bus to Charlotte, North Carolina, to meet with the Army physician. She met the age requirement which was between 21 and 45. Next, a woman had to stand at least 60 inches tall. Ruth was 63 inches.

The weight requirement proved a problem. A WAAC had to weigh at least 105 pounds. When Ruth stood on the scale in the doctor's office, the pointer tipped to 98 pounds.

"Eat bananas, drink milk, and come back another time," advised the physician, shooing Ruth out of his office.

She walked outside, wanting to stomp her foot. It was too inconvenient to make a return trip to Charlotte for another exam.

Ruth entered a diner across the street where she ordered a hearty meal. After dining, she returned to the doctor's office. Ruth must have looked determined because the doctor took one look and ushered her inside. Without a word, wearing her coat and shoes and holding her purse which was stuffed with rocks, she stepped on the scale.

The scale tipped at the 105-pound mark.

The physician signed the form before stopping Ruth before she left the office. "Do you really want to join the Army?" he asked.

"Yes." She had chosen this way to help her country. She would pursue it with everything in her.

A few weeks after submitting her application, a letter from the Army arrived, stating that Ruth had been accepted into the WAACs.

In March 1943, she boarded a bus at Marion for basic training. Her suitcase contained only a few personal items. No civilian clothing, other than those she wore, was needed.

Neither Ruth, nor the other women on the bus who were also new recruits, knew where they were headed. Wherever it was, they were going together.

The group disembarked at Fort Oglethorpe, Georgia. The next six weeks meant rising at 0600 hours each day to dress and fall out for roll call. They marched to a field for physical training drills before later attending courses on map reading, defense against chemical warfare and air attacks, military customs, and courtesy.

The recruits ate in a cavernous building called the mess hall. Sometimes the WAACs were called for K.P. (Kitchen Police) duty. One part of K.P. Ruth detested was cleaning grease traps. Once, her cleaning job didn't pass inspection and she had to do it over.

The women slept in barracks lined with rows of bunks. Each WAAC was taught responsibility in caring for issued items -- Army blanket, sheets, pillow, footlocker placed at the base of the bed, and wall locker. Everything had a place and nothing lay around.

On Saturday mornings the WAACs stood for formal inspection. Officers walked down the aisles of the barrack, checking each woman's appearance and area. A bed had to be made so tightly that a quarter bounced on it. If a bed failed inspection, its occupant was gigged – punished—and made to do it over. Ruth was careful never to have that happen.

They stood at attention, hands at their sides, answering any question asked of them. The WAACs never looked at the officers or questioned them. Ruth enjoyed the orderliness and always passed inspection.

When basic training was completed, the WAACs were split up and sent to their first assignments. Ruth had volunteered to go overseas. Instead, she was sent to Kelly Field in San Antonio. Other WAACs worked on bases around the United States.

After traveling by train overnight to Kelly, Ruth was assigned to managing rosters at base headquarters (HQ). This included keeping track of paperwork for officers' transfers and those headed overseas.

Ruth worked five days a week, 0800 hours to 1600 hours. Her assignment at HQ earned her the rank of corporal and later, sergeant. She was proud of the three stripes on her cotton uniform. She still had to stand for inspection and observe rules of service like the other WAACs. Her pay was $78 a month.

By August 1943, 60,000 women served the WAAC program. It was not enough.

On August 31, 1943, the WAAC service disbanded and all of the WAAC's were dismissed. The following day, the Women's Army Corps (WAC) was formed. Former WAACs were encouraged to re-enlist with the assurance that those who did would be sworn in with full military status and benefits. More than 45,000 WAACs re-enlisted, including Ruth Cooper. Recruitment efforts were stepped up around the country to increase enlistments.

With basic training completed, Ruth had more time for fun. She joined the softball team where she played shortstop. Movie theaters, swimming pools, and tennis courts on base were available to the women for recreation when off-duty. The WACs could also play cards in the base's day room or take judo lessons. On occasion the WACs received leave to visit San Antonio.

On Sundays, Ruth attended the Protestant chapel on base where she sang in the choir. The base had chapels for all denominations.

In an effort to further increase morale and boost recruitments, a contest was held in fall 1943 on San Antonio-area air field bases to recognize the WACs. In particular, the military wanted to recognize a certain group of women who, according to WAC commanders as quoted in San Antonio newspapers, 'embodied the idea of a female counterpart to the male soldier – someone who was willing to work hard, sacrificially, and with little fuss.'

One woman from each participating base would be chosen and recognized with the name of 'Miss Victory.' Ruth was shocked when the WACs at Kelly Field voted her 'Miss Victory'.

Three WACs from Hondo, Brooks, and Randolph Army Fields, were voted 'Miss Victory' at their bases. These four representatives would be guests of honor at a ball scheduled for December 13, 1943.

Festivities in preparation for the ball began a week earlier when 'Army Air Forces Salute the WAC Day' was proclaimed nationally by Major General Barney M. Giles, chief of the Air Staff. More than 150 air force installations around the country paid tribute to uniformed women.

On the evening of December 13, Ruth and the other Miss Victorys arrived at Municipal Auditorium in San Antonio with their respective dates. Thousands of enlisted men and women from fields throughout the San Antonio area attended to salute the work of the WACs.

The four Miss Victorys opened the event by leading a grand march. During the formal ceremony at the ball, Major General Gerald C. Brant, commanding general of the AAF Central Flying Training Command, pinned flowers on each of the four women. He also presented them with individual bracelets and trophies engraved with their names, the words 'Miss Victory', and Air Force wings on them.

Ruth's trophy -- and possibly the trophies of the other Miss Victorys -- stayed at the base on display. Years later, Ruth would give her bracelet to a daughter.

The nationally acclaimed singing trio, The Andrews Sisters, and the San Antonio Aviation Cadet Center Skyline Patrol Orchestra performed musical selections. It was a lovely evening, one that Ruth would remember all of her life.

In actuality, rules for dating at Kelly Field were stringent. If a WAC went on a date, she told the young man good-bye at the base's gate. The WACs could bring men to the base only by permission.

Ruth did date several young men. But only one attracted her serious attention.

In June 1944, while on a blind date, Ruth met Tech Sergeant Bill Licking. A native of Greensburg,

Indiana, he had been stationed in Panama for three years and was now at Kelly Field in an administrative position.

Ruth enjoyed Bill's company and good manners. He confessed he got a charge from her southern accent. He also liked her brown eyes and blond hair.

During the next several months, the two went out almost every night, either to movies or a dance. By December, Ruth was sure Bill was the man she wanted to marry. When he proposed, she accepted.

They were married on February 17, 1945, at the base chapel. Chaplain John K. Roberts performed the ceremony. Lieutenant Colonel Andrew J. Curbo, Jr. gave Ruth away. Her roommate was the maid of honor, while Bill's best friend from Panama volunteered as best man.

Due to gas shortages and difficulty in travel, neither families of the bride and groom attended, though they sent telegrams of well-wishes. The church was full with friends from the base.

Ruth wore a floor-length white wedding dress loaned to her by another WAC. She carried a bouquet of white camellias and narcissus. Bill's gold wedding band, which cost Ruth $45, was engraved with their names and wedding date.

Ruth's office staff gave the couple a set of linens with the words 'Marching Along Together' printed in red cursive on top.

After hosting a dinner for the wedding party, Mr. and Mrs. Licking drove to Austin for a three-day honeymoon. They borrowed a car.

When Ruth was discharged from the Army in September 1945, she waited until Bill was discharged a month later. Then they headed to Greensburg, Indiana, so Ruth could meet his family. They became parents to four children and moved to Bluffton, Indiana, to open a men's clothing store.

Her thoughts: "In the Army we were told there were two ways to live – our way and the Army way. I was happy as a soldier living the Army way. If anybody would ask me to do it again, I would. I might not have done as much for my country as an American soldier stationed overseas, but I filled a gap. As little as it might have been, I helped."

Ruth Cooper Licking was voted 'Miss Victory' by other WACs for exemplifying ideal WAC qualities of a hard work ethic and willingness to sacrifice without fuss.

Bonnie Calhoun Neuenschwander Habegger

Army Nurse Corps

As the eldest of 10 children, Bonnie Calhoun of Kaufman, Texas, grew up learning how to care for her siblings' many illnesses and injuries. Bonnie found she enjoyed caring for people with physical hurts. Those experiences kindled something deep inside her – she wanted to be a nurse.

Born in 1923, Bonnie and her large family learned how to make money stretch during the Great Depression of the 1930s.

After graduating from Kaufman High School in 1941, Bonnie scraped together enough money to attend two years of nursing school.

She worked two years with the training she had. Then in 1945, Bonnie heard about a program that could help her earn a degree.

The Army was recruiting women for its nursing corps. The Army would pay for expenses like books, tuition, and lodging. In return, the women would enlist for a designated amount of time, including after the war ended.

Bonnie Calhoun immediately enlisted. Like her male counterparts, she had to complete basic training. This included learning to march to meals, performing daily calisthenics, saluting and standing at attention, as well as Army protocol and procedures.

Upon graduating in May 1945, Second Lieutenant Bonnie Calhoun immediately began her work at a military hospital in San Antonio. There, she saw some of the war's worst ravages with wounded soldiers shipped home, shrapnel trapped throughout their bodies, burns, frostbite, and more.

Later, she was transferred to McCloskey General Hospital in Temple, Texas, and Dallas Methodist Hospital. In both locations Bonnie cared for soldiers with lost limbs and other ailments.

When the Army asked for volunteers to go overseas to help the wounded in Europe, 22-year-old Bonnie thought about the request. The war in Europe had ended with a German surrender. Many men, injured during battles late in the war, lay in hospital beds. Nurses were needed to help them heal and go home.

The idea of being so far from home made Bonnie anxious. She had been raised in church and believed in praying about every decision and searched her Bible for answers. After a few weeks, she felt God was calling her to serve overseas.

Bonnie sailed on the SS *John Ericsson* to Bremerhaven, Germany, thankful not to suffer from seasickness during the two-week voyage.

From Bremerhaven she traveled to Mourmelon, France, where she was put in charge of a ward at a station hospital.

Bonnie and other nurses had been warned about some of the soldiers' eagerness to see women. Hospital protocol stated that nurses would always enter wards accompanied by military guards.

As she had in the United States, Bonnie Calhoun established her own rules of behavior with male patients. She didn't like dirty jokes. If a soldier said something nasty, she threatened to walk away, pain meds in tow. The bad language stopped.

On Sundays, she attended church services at the base chapel. A young soldier named Howard Neuenschwander led the singing. He was from Berne, Indiana, and served as the chaplain's assistant.

Since she had been a teen, Bonnie had asked God to provide her with a Christian husband. She had no thought of falling in love while in the military and was not looking for a beau while serving as a nurse in Europe.

However, when, one night after chapel services ended, Howard Neuenschwander asked Bonnie if he could walk her to her room, she consented. She was impressed with his good manners and neat appearance.

But there was a problem.

Army protocol forbade officers like Bonnie from fraternizing with (dating) enlisted personnel. When another nurse had dated an enlisted soldier, the Army assigned them to different bases.

In compliance with the non-fraternization rule, Bonnie spent off-duty time in the ice cream parlor where Howard was in charge. He also managed the post exchange (PX), a store on the base.

While eating ice cream, the pair chatted. Bonnie found Howard fun and interesting. Sometimes they took a chance of receiving reprimands to meet at movie theaters, hoping in the darkened theaters their ranks could not be detected.

When, after four months, Bonnie received orders for a transfer to the 120th Station Hospital in Bayreuth, Germany, she felt sad at leaving Howard. Even during a short leave to Paris, she looked forward to seeing him upon her return.

Then Howard received his discharge orders, guaranteeing a permanent separation. The couple vowed to write letters.

In truth, Bonnie had little time to think of romance in Bayreuth, as she was head nurse on a hospital prison ward. She supervised five enlisted men who helped in caring for 30 patients. They were American soldiers who had allegedly committed crimes and somehow incurred injuries that warranted hospitalization.

Bonnie and her ward men were not allowed to talk to the prisoners about why they had been arrested. The prisoners were constantly under the watch of military guards.

Some German citizens worked at the hospital. In Bonnie's opinion, their attitudes towards the Americans post-war was for the most part respectful. She had no trouble from them.

Off-duty, Bonnie enjoyed the village of Bayreuth. It was located in the Bavarian region world-famous for its music, mainly centered on its hometown native and 19th-century composer, Richard Wagner. Each day at mealtime a cellist, violinist, and pianist came to the hospital to play classical music. Their selections usually included his operas. From this influence Bonnie developed a love for classical music which she carried with her after the war.

During the summer of 1945, scuttlebutt (nickname for military gossip) spread about plans for a major Allied invasion in Japan to help end the war. Nurses would be vitally needed as projected casualties were reported to be in the millions.

Bonnie tried to prepare herself emotionally and mentally for this possibility. Again, the young Texan woman prayed about her decision and sought her Bible for answers. What more might be required of her in service to her country?

When the Japanese surrendered and the war ended, Bonnie was one of millions of people worldwide who celebrated in great relief.

First Lieutenant Bonnie Calhoun (she had been promoted) was honorably discharged on June 15, 1946. She had been in Germany for 13 months.

After sailing home across the Atlantic, Bonnie arrived at Boston Harbor and made her way to the Midwest. She wanted to visit Howard in Berne.

During their separation, the pair had written many letters to each other. Though she had dated other people, Bonnie never found anyone she cared for like Howard. He felt the same for her. Their time apart had cemented their love.

They were married in October 1946 at Bonnie's home in Texas. She moved to Berne where Howard founded an insurance business with his brother. They raised four children and Bonnie working in private duty nursing.

After Howard died in 1986, Bonnie married Grant Habegger, another World War II veteran from Berne.

Her thoughts: "I had a good experience in the military. I enjoyed my work and had fun. I was happy to serve my country. I did my duty and felt needed."

Bonnie Calhoun Neuenschwander Habegger served as a nurse in France and Germany.

Mary 'Polly' Woodhull Lipscomb

Army Nurse Corps

During the Revolutionary War, Abraham Woodhull was a spy for General George Washington, providing information on the British Army. One hundred and sixty years later, during another war, a female descendent would reflect his patriotic spirit in helping her country.

Mary Adelaide 'Polly' Woodhull was born in Ann Arbor, Michigan, in 1913. After her family moved to Fort Wayne, Indiana, for her father's job at Magnavox, Polly earned a degree from International Business College.

But when she began searching for a job, Samuel forbade her from doing so. It was during the Great Depression and jobs were hard to find. Samuel felt Polly would be taking a job from a man who needed it to support a family.

So Polly chose a different career, one more acceptable for women at that time -- nursing.

After earning a degree from Methodist Hospital in Fort Wayne in 1936, Polly worked at hospitals in California and the Richardson House in Boston before returning to Fort Wayne to work in general practice for Dr. Carl G. Miller.

After hearing about the Japanese bombing of Pearl Harbor in December 1941, Dr. Miller closed his office to enlist. Polly followed suit by enlisting in the Army Nurse Corps in August 1942.

Polly was not the only Woodhull to fight in WWII. Her brother Charles enlisted in the Navy, while another brother, Ben, joined the Army Air Corps. Youngest brother Sam volunteered as a cadet in the Civil Air Patrol.

Second Lieutenant Polly Woodhull and other Army nurses completed three months of training at Fort Knox in Kentucky before being transferred to Camp Kilmer, New Jersey. They had been chosen to meet the quota of nurses needed overseas.

The night before she was due to leave, a soldier arrived at Polly's room to stencil her baggage with name, serial, and shipping numbers. He had to complete the process for each nurse. The soldier looked tired so Polly offered him a glass of tea and suggested she do her own stencils. He accepted the offers gratefully.

Each nurse's duffel bag held bed roll, helmet, gas mask, and backpack. They could not take civilian clothing. The next morning when they boarded the

Queen Mary, the nurses had no idea where they were being sent.

The Queen Mary was a former luxury ship converted to troop ship. It was considered the fastest in the world. As it could avoid German submarines that patrolled the Atlantic, the vessel did not observe zig-zag procedures, which most troop ships performed for evasion. The captain still observed precautionary practices by ordering all of the ship's windows to be blacked out. As a further precaution, no one was allowed to stand on deck after dark.

Polly and the nurses were housed nine to a room with bunk beds. There was no private bathroom or fresh water, forcing the women to bathe in sticky salt water.

When the ship arrived a week later at the British Isles, Polly was assigned to the 67th General Hospital in the village of Taunton, about 100 miles southwest of London. The 67th was a set of new buildings made of brick and stone. It was designated for Allied troops: British, Canadian, and American. Local civilians also received medical treatment at the hospital.

The 67th's patients arrived via trains and ambulances from station hospitals on battlefields across the English Channel. It was always hectic at the hospital when the patients arrived.

Some patients' injuries were slight and they could be returned to their units. Others with badly damaged limbs from shrapnel or frostbite were sent back to the United States.

American Colonel Roland B. Moore was in charge of the 67th. During World War I, he had served as assistant surgeon of the 76th Division in France. Captain Marjorie P. French had charge of the 67th's nursing staff.

The 67th had many wards, including surgery, ear, nose, throat, orthopedic, physical therapy, psychiatric, and a prison ward.

The British system of addressing nurses was the word 'Sisters'. The head nurse was 'Matron'. Polly and the Americans adapted to the new monikers.

A military base post office, barracks, laundry, and post exchange completed the complex.

In the American nurses' quarters Polly had a room to herself equipped with bed, dresser, and closet.

While overall Polly was pleased with the hospital, she did have a couple of criticisms. From patient comments she learned the 36 beds in her ward were too small and uncomfortable.

Her other complaint was the chilly temperatures in the hospital. While a few wards had steam heat, most were warmed solely by pot belly stoves placed in the middle of bed rows.

The nurses' quarters were just as sparsely heated. During winter, the women sat wrapped in woolly government-issued sweaters and blankets, their stockinged feet resting on the small pipe filled with warm water that ran down the middle of the room for heat.

Enlisted men who worked at the hospital had it worse with only one small potbelly stove per tent. Each man was issued a blanket and overcoat, the latter of which they usually wore to bed.

The nursing staff was assisted by four American Red Cross women who read letters to patients and located toothpaste and razors for shaving. Villagers knitted blankets and stockings.

When the Red Cross hosted dances, Polly attended. She enjoyed camaraderie with the British people.

But no one ever forgot there was a war on.

When air raid sirens occurred at night for drills, the hospital staff – whether on duty or off – had to report to the area where they had worked the day before.

They donned gas masks and helmets and waited until the 'all clear' was given. At that point it was back to bed or duty. The drills could occur multiple times a night. Participation was required.

Polly was thankful the hospital was never bombed, although on occasion she did see flak in the air from enemy planes. She admired the B-17s, nicknamed 'Flying Fortresses' because of their size and firing power capability. She often stopped to watch as they flew over the hospital headed for the English Channel and targets in Europe.

As her eyes scanned the skies, Polly wondered if her brother, Ben, was inside one of them. She knew from his letters that he was stationed somewhere in England with the Army Air Corps.

One military protocol at the hospital was never interrupted for the war – weekly inspections. Each Saturday morning, high-ranking officers examined everything from patients' beds to the kitchen area, windows, even baseboards. Everything had to be immaculate. If a ward did not pass inspection, the person in charge received a verbal reprimand.

Ambulatory patients often helped the medical staff to prepare for an inspection. One patient chose to sleep under his bed to keep its neat appearance until the inspection was over.

Another reminder of the war was the blackouts. Since the war had begun for England in 1939, it had enforced blackouts at night. Every window was covered by heavy curtains. Neighborhood wardens kept an eye on all buildings for gaps of light. The goal was to have no crack of light showing that could give the Germans a target.

Many buildings were adapted with two sets of front doors. Upon entering the outermost door, a person shut it securely before opening the next.

No street lights meant people walking at night could bump into a pole or another person. Car headlights showed just enough light to get by.

Polly learned lessons about the British and their resilience when her first batch of wounded soldiers arrived shortly after her arrival. They had fought in the Battle of Oran Harbor in Algeria.

When a 22-year-old soldier had his left leg amputated above the knee, Polly grieved for him. He surprised her by telling her he wanted a dance.

The British people also rallied at the enforced rationing, also put into effect in 1939. They had adapted by cutting back on a myriad of items, including milk, fruit, eggs, candy, gum, soap, cigarettes, canned fruit juice, toilet paper, gasoline, paper, rubber for tires.

The only available bread was dark because there was no white flour. Coffee -- some sort of chicory –

was plentiful, as was tea, though the latter had a strong taste.

An alternative to fresh eggs was the powder form. Polly disliked the rubbery taste. Once, when an enlisted soldier who was dating an English woman brought a fresh egg from her farm to the hospital, Polly and a few members of the staff fried it and shared it so each person had a bite.

When Polly hired an elderly woman to do her laundry, she saw more of the British people's fortitude. On the nights she retrieved her items at their cottage, 'Mum' and 'Pop' Payne, as they wanted to be called, invited her to sit and chat over a cup of tea. The three huddled close to the fireplace, covered with coats and blankets, as the couple's tiny bit of rationed coal put out a meager heat.

When members of the 67th staff was given fresh oranges. Polly kept hers for a week, whiffing its fresh scent daily, before finally eating it.

As Polly had worked in psychiatric wards in the States, she was assigned to that type of ward at one point at the 67th. Many patients suffered from what was termed 'shell shock'. Note: In the 21st century, a soldier diagnosed with similar combat-related symptoms might be diagnosed with 'post-traumatic stress.'

Nurses assigned to the psychiatric unit were trained to assist patients diagnosed with severe illnesses like schizophrenia. Agitated patients might be sedated.

Some patients found comfort in crafts. The nurses showed them how to stay calm with the repetitive, gentle movement of weaving using the hospital's loom. When a soldier gave Polly an orange scarf he had made, she treasured it throughout her life.

In December 1942, the mayor of Taunton sent invitations to American medical personnel at the 67th for a Christmas reception and dance. Polly and the other nurses who attended thought it was a lovely event which they enjoyed immensely.

On Christmas Day, Captain French cooked breakfast for her female officers. Then, Polly worked in her ward before helping the Red Cross women decorate the enlisted men's mess hall. That evening, enlisted men, officers, and doctors ate together. It was a busy, fun day.

In the spring, Polly borrowed a bicycle on her days off to ride through the beautiful English countryside viewing houses with thatched roofs. The roads were dotted with people on bikes. British cars traveled on the left side of roads so she had to be careful.

Occasionally, American nurses rode trains to London during their leaves. Air raid sirens often interrupted their quest for entertainment, forcing the Americans to follow Londoners headed to the closest subway for protection.

Despite air raids at the hospital, rationing, and threats of bombs, Polly was not scared or even homesick. When she was sitting at a concert and heard the national anthem of the 'Star-Spangled Banner' playing for Americans in the audience, her eyes welled with tears of pride. She served a great country.

It wasn't long before the people at the 67th and Taunton became her second family.

Polly had another reason for not being homesick. She had fallen in love.

Several weeks after arriving in England, Polly attended a USO party. She noticed the soldier who had offered to stencil her bags at Camp Kilmer. Recalling his friendly demeanor, she approached him and re-introduced herself.

Tech Corporal Alexander Hughston Lipscomb – Alec was the name he preferred -- smiled and said he remembered her. When he asked her to dance, she agreed.

As they moved about the floor, he explained that he had grown up on a farm near Tulsa, Oklahoma. After being drafted into the Army, he was sent to England where he was assigned as a driver to the 67th's medivac ambulance service. Afterward, Alec drove her and other nurses back to their barracks in his assigned truck.

The next day, Polly's superior female officer reprimanded her for fraternizing with an enlisted soldier. She reminded Polly that it was against Army protocol for officers.

Polly listened quietly. Then she informed her superior that she would rather fraternize with an *un*married enlisted man than with a married officer. Her superior knew Polly was referring to her.

Likewise, Alec was reprimanded for spending time with an officer. Their warnings went unheeded.

During the next several months, Alec and Polly met in dark movie theaters where people could not see stripes on their uniforms. Sometimes they borrowed bikes to ride in the country or rode buses to tour other towns.

The American nurse and Oklahoma cowboy could not have been more different in backgrounds and personalities. But Polly enjoyed Alec's company.

Things were going well until Polly was assigned a new duty, one that nearly derailed the couple's relationship for good.

Each piece of American military personal correspondence was read by censors on the base from which it originated. These censors – all military personnel -- carefully blacked out any words or phrases that relayed information about the Allied war effort.

When Polly was assigned to read mail sent from the 67th's motor pool, she didn't anticipate reading letters written by Alec Lipscomb to females in California and Oklahoma.

She knew he was a healthy 28-year-old American male. What she didn't realize was how popular he was with women back home.

What really annoyed Polly was that the letters were filled with 'one-liners' – statements Alec had created that he felt succinctly conveyed his sentiments. Often, the same one-liner was sent to each female correspondent.

Polly recognized the one-liners for what they were. Alec had often repeated them to her. He even confessed he and his tent-mates worked together at night to create the statements for their girlfriends.

One day, while walking together, Polly began reciting the one-liners to Alec. He was startled. Some of them were knew and he knew he had not yet said them to her.

When Polly explained about her position as censor for his department, he was incensed. He arranged to have his letters read by a different censor.

Despite this hiccup in the couple's relationship, they became closer. Alec stopped writing letters to the other women and by summer 1945, he had proposed. Polly accepted.

They were married on August 19, 1945, at Independent Congregational Chapel, Salisbury Street, Blandford, County of Dorset.

An Army chaplain conducted the ceremony. Pop Payne walked Polly down the aisle. An Army friend was Polly's maid of honor, while Alec's friend, Virgil Rust, served as best man. Lacking a wedding dress or any civilian clothes, Polly wore her uniform.

The couple obtained leave for a week's honeymoon along the Torquay coast. Then it was back to work for both of them.

When the Japanese emperor surrendered on August 14, 1945 ('Victory in Japan', VJ Day), Polly and Alec made plans for their new lives together.

Before Polly and some other nurses left England, they were served an elegant formal dinner with blueberry pie for dessert by the hospital. It left a pleasant memory of England with the nurses.

In September, Polly and Alec sailed home on the Queen Elizabeth. American authorities had accepted their British marriage license, but the military still insisted they could not spend time together on the ship. The married couple renewed their skills of evasion by meeting in dark corners and under stairways.

When the majestic ship arrived in New York Harbor, military police finally allowed Polly and Alec to stand together at the rail to view the Statue of Liberty. A band on shore played 'Beer Barrel Polka' to welcome the soldiers home.

The Lipscombs were separated yet again as each had to re-join their respective military units to receive their discharges. First Lieutenant Polly Lipscomb was discharged at Fort Sheridan in Illinois. Alec Lipscomb headed to Fort Bliss in Texas and was later discharged at Camp Atterbury in southern Indiana.

As there was not much family of Alec's family or work in Oklahoma, he and Polly lived near her family in Fort Wayne. All of Polly's brothers returned home safely.

Polly and Alec became parents to three children. Alec worked as a mechanic. When their children were older, Polly resumed her nursing career.

Their son, Sam, continued the family's military tradition by serving with the Army 1967-1970. In 2002, grandson Army Second Lieutenant Jason Lipscomb went into the Iraq invasion as a rifle platoon leader wearing Polly's officer bars. A granddaughter, Sergeant Janeen Lipscomb Wilch, followed her grandmother's example by serving as a nurse in the Army.

Shortly after arriving in Taunton in December 1942, Polly reflected her ancestral patriotic spirit when she wrote these words in a letter to her parents: "I'm happy to be here to help a little bit for the good old US and the American flag that we Americans are so proud to see over here."

Polly Woodhull Lipscomb died on June 4, 10 days before her 102nd birthday.

Mary 'Polly' Woodhull Lipscomb served as a nurse in England, during which time she married a soldier.

Doris Eileen Stuckey Zeissig
Army Nurse Corps

While listening to a radio in the break room of Lutheran Hospital in Fort Wayne on December 7, 1941, Doris Eileen Stuckey was stunned to hear the horrifying news of Pearl Harbor.

Eileen, as she preferred to be called, and the medical staff had never heard of Pearl Harbor. Still, they understood it was a horrible event with far-reaching repercussions.

Eileen had been born in Berne, Indiana, in 1921. Upon graduating from Berne High School in 1939, she was uncertain of a career. A visit to Riley Children's Hospital in Indianapolis changed that. Eileen wanted to be a nurse.

The first year's tuition to nursing school was steep: $125. But she managed to pay for it and graduated in 1943 before working for a year at a local hospital.

The war had dragged on. Eileen Stuckey, like most Americans, wanted to help.

In June 1944, the Allies completed the largest sea invasion the world has ever known at Normandy, France. That same month Eileen decided to join the

Army and work as a nurse to help wounded servicemen.

At the beginning of World War II, the only American women allowed to wear uniforms were members of the Army Nurse Corps and Navy Nurse Corps. By the end of World War II, 57,000 women would join the Army Nurse Corps.

When Eileen left home, her parents put a banner with four blue stars in their front window. Their daughter and three sons were serving in the military. Eileen knew her parents prayed for everyone's safe return.

As a college graduate, Eileen Stuckey was commissioned as an officer at the rank of second lieutenant. Her salary in the Army was $150.00 per month. With those funds she was responsible for buying her own uniforms, which consisted of white one-piece dresses and white shoes. Off-duty, Army nurses still had to wear military clothing, such as olive-colored dress uniforms.

Eileen worked at a military hospital at Fort Benjamin Harrison in Indianapolis before being sent to Ashford General Hospital at White Sulphur Springs, West Virginia.

The elegant resort with velvet curtains had been converted to a hospital. Eileen worked on various wards, including general nursing, paraplegic, and post-op. When trains brought in the wounded shipped home from overseas, the hospital staff scrambled to accommodate the needs. Nurses, billeted in small cottages on the estate, worked 12-hour shifts with one weekend off per month.

Eileen enjoyed her work and the surroundings. But in May 1945, when the call to serve as a nurse overseas was announced, she volunteered to go. She sailed for Europe on a ship that landed in Scotland before venturing down to England.

On May 8th, Germany had signed a formal surrender to the Allies. The war in Europe was over, but thousands of casualties required care throughout the continent.

Eileen worked at a hospital on England's south coast before she was transferred to a hospital in Reims, France – the city where the war's formal surrender had taken place in a schoolhouse a few months earlier.

Next, Eileen traveled to Bad Mergentheim, Germany, where she worked at an evacuation hospital near the former frontlines.

Eileen had heard about the planned Allied invasion of Japan. She braced herself for orders to be sent to that country. The number of estimated deaths from the invasion were one million. Eileen shuddered.

Then on August 8, 1945, the unexpected occurred -- Japan surrendered! The formal surrender took place on September 14, 1945, on the USS *Missouri* in Tokyo Bay. The date became known as Victory in Japan Day, or 'VJ' Day.

People around the world celebrated the war's end. Eileen's parents could look forward to seeing their four children again.

Some people had even more reasons to celebrate the war's end. Sergeant Leslie Stuckey, one of Eileen's brothers, had been stationed at Norwich, England with the Eighth Air Force. He had fallen in love with an English female pilot. They planned to marry in England.

The couple invited Eileen to attend their wedding. After receiving permission from her commanding officer to go, Eileen rode a train to Norwich.

It was a simple wedding officiated by a clerk. At the reception the hotel served fish and chips (rationing of meat and other foodstuffs would continue until the 1950s).

After a few hours, Eileen and Leslie excused themselves to take a walk. As they strolled down a street, they chatted about their service, their brothers, and what life would be like after the war.

Suddenly, they were stopped by an American military police (MP) officer. When he told the pair they could not be together as that was fraternizing, they smiled and showed him their dog tags.

When the MP was convinced they were related, he apologized. Leslie invited him to the reception and the young officer accepted. From what Eileen could tell, he enjoyed himself.

Eileen's next assignment was vastly different from anything she had done before. She had read a notice asking nurses to help in a nursery of 100 babies belonging to French women who had married American servicemen. The babies and their mothers would sail soon for the States.

Eileen signed up to accompany the group to their new home in America.

In June 1946, First Lieutenant Stuckey was discharged in New Jersey. She rode a train to Fort Wayne where she was picked up by her mother and taken to her home in Berne.

Eileen was glad to be home. She returned to Lutheran Hospital where she was offered a position in surgery.

In 1947, Eileen Stuckey married Master Sergeant Werner Zeissig from Fort Wayne. He had spent five years in the Army Air Corps stationed in England. The couple became parents to five children. Eileen worked in private duty nursing for much of her life.

One of her greatest privileges was laying a wreath on the Tomb of the Unknown Soldier during an Honor Flight of Northeast Indiana in 2014.

Her thoughts: "It was a privilege to care for our wounded soldiers. I only wish we could have had today's medical technology. We could have saved an awful lot more lives."

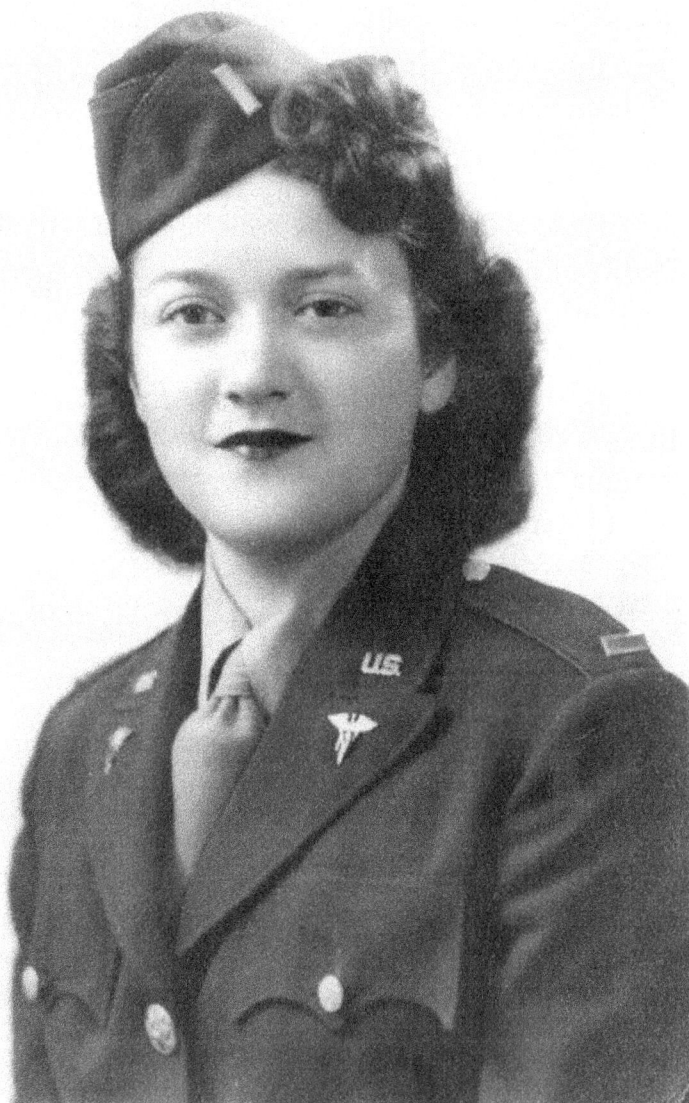

Doris 'Eileen' Stuckey Zeissig served in hospitals in France and Germany while stationed in Europe.

Women Accepted for Volunteer Emergency Service

Rose Mary Anderson Flener

After graduating from Concannon High School in Terre Haute, Indiana, in 1942, Rose Mary Anderson found a job at the Terre Haute Ordinance Depot (a military supply station). The eldest of five children in her family, Rose Mary knew she had a responsibility to help add to the family's income.

She typed bills of lading for jeeps, all-terrain vehicles, and other military equipment that were transported across the country. Rose Mary enjoyed her work, but she was also worried.

While growing up, Rose Mary and her family had spent time socializing with a family named Flener. One evening, 18-year-old Rose Mary had attended a carnival with the Anderson's son, Richard. He was two years older.

The two began dating. Rose Mary and Richard fell in love shortly before he was drafted into the Army in November 1942. When he left for the South Pacific, Rose Mary tried not to think that she may never see him again. She wanted to do something to help the war effort. She decided to join the WAVES.

Rose Mary chose that branch of the military because a female cousin had joined the WACs. Rose Mary learned the WACs were sometimes sent overseas. Her recruiter assured Rose Mary that WAVES never left the United States.

Rose Mary loved her family and wanted to be available in case of emergency. At the same time, she looked forward to seeing the country. Her parents, Joseph and Lulu Anderson, had owned a general store which was open every day of week. This arrangement offered no opportunity for them to get away for a vacation. Rose Mary believed adventures awaited her in the WAVES.

A couple of obstacles threatened her plans.

The military stated that if a woman was not age 21, a parent had to give written permission for her to join the military. Rose Mary would turn 20 years old on March 23, 1944, the date on which she wanted to enlist. She asked Joseph Anderson to give his written permission. Her father resisted, saying he didn't believe women – in particular, his daughter -- should be in the military.

Lulu Anderson felt no reticence in allowing her daughter to become a member of the Navy. She told

Joseph, "If you don't sign the paper, I will." He signed the form.

Then, another larger obstacle presented itself. During Rose Mary's physical exam for the military, she was found to have poor oral health, in particular her teeth were in bad shape.

Rose Mary's dentist pulled one tooth so that she could pass the exam. When he recommended treatment to mend other problems (he suspected she had a gum disease), Rose Mary protested. The treatment would take more time than she was allowed before leaving with the Navy.

Rose Mary's dentist capitulated, although he strongly urged her to visit a military dentist as soon as she got to boot camp. She promised to do so.

Before Rose Mary left for Hunter College in May 1944, she received a letter from Richard who, like Joseph, said he didn't want her to enlist. Rose Mary was determined to be a WAVES and left for Hunter College.

Rose Mary and a thousand other WAVES recruits arrived for six weeks of boot camp in late spring. The rainy season forced the women to wear military rain gear and havelock (head gear) with long flaps while learning to march and drill.

During their last weekend, the WACs were given passes to visit New York City. Full of excitement, Rose Mary and her friends toured the Statue of Liberty and Empire State Building, then the world's tallest building. They ate at the famous, elegant Waldorf Astoria where Rose Mary believed they were served a great meal at reasonable prices.

She was happy to learn that of the all of the WAVES who went into the city, only one failed to return to the college by curfew on Sunday evening.

As another reward for finishing boot camp, the WAVES were allowed to call home -- the first time since saying good-bye to their families. During the call, they informed their families of their first assignments.

Rose Mary told her parents that she was being sent to Agricultural & Mechanical (A&M) College at Stillwater, Oklahoma, for studies as a yeoman.

Until she heard her parents' voices, Rose Mary hadn't realized how homesick she was. Still, she grew excited to think about the next chapter in her military life that would take place in a new part of the country.

But, again, her dental condition threatened her plans. Rose Mary had not kept her promise to visit the military dentist soon after arriving at Hunter, fearing she would be sent home. Instead, she saw him during her last week.

He scolded her for waiting as she now had swollen, red, and tender gums. The dentist diagnosed it as a serious gum infection called pyorrhea. The disease would later be referred to as periodontitis.

When the dentist tried to treat the pyorrhea with painful medicine on Rose Mary's gums, it failed to work.

As boot camp was almost over and Rose Mary was being shipped to another base, the dentist gave her a similar warning to what she had received from her dentist at home -- she should see the base dentist at her new assignment as soon as she arrived. She again promised to do so.

At Grand Central Station Rose Mary and the other WAVES boarded a train headed west to their various destinations. During the next several days, the women billeted not in fancy sleeper cars, but on triple-decked bunks inside boxcars. During the long trip, the women varied their surroundings by eating in the dining car.

Upon the train making a routine stop in St. Louis, Missouri, the women disembarked to find a pleasant surprise. Residents ushered them to an area set up with tables laden with food. The WAVES were offered the sumptuous feast in thanks for their service. It was a tribute the people of St. Louis gave to other troop trains which stopped while heading to destinations throughout the country.

When an Army troop train pulled in at the same time, its soldiers exited to the sight of the young WAVES and home baked goods. The men eagerly took seats at the tables and for a brief while, young people from around the country enjoyed the camaraderie of others intent on serving their country at war.

When the train whistle sounded, the groups dispersed, full of homecooked food and memories of laughter and conversation with strangers.

The train pulled into the station at Stillwater late in the day. Rose Mary and the other WAVES assigned to A&M College were taken to what she thought was an attractive dorm on an equally beautiful campus. She didn't mind billeting with another WAVES on the top floor.

Rose Mary was especially impressed with the food served in the dining hall. Since A&M was an agricultural college, fresh vegetables, dairy, and meat were plentiful at each meal. The menu often included peppermint ice cream as the college grew plants from which they made syrup.

The women took courses in history and Navy protocol, while continuing to march and drill. Rose Mary especially enjoyed history class. Their male instructor began each class as though he was a radio announcer (there was no TV), presenting news on the war and identifying countries on a map.

Each night the women studied for exams in their rooms. At mail call, women gathered outside of Rose Mary's door to see if she had received a package. Lulu Anderson often sent cheese, canned meat, crackers, and cookies, which Rose Mary shared.

She kept her promise to visit the base dentist at Stillwater. When the pyorrhea did not respond to treatment, the dentist believed the only solution was to extract all of Rose Mary's teeth.

It was an arduous ordeal. Once the task was completed, Rose Mary was instructed to go to the kitchen on the lower level to get herself an ice pack.

Feeling woozy, she obeyed. By the time she returned, she was nearly in shock. The medical staff gave her a sedative, then covered her with blankets and assigned a nurse to watch her during the night.

By morning, Rose Mary felt better. The plan was that after healing for a few days, the Navy would send her to Norman Oklahoma Naval Hospital to be fitted with dentures.

At the accorded time, Rose Mary boarded an interurban train for Norman. When she exited the dentist office with her new teeth, she spied five friends waiting for her with a wheelchair. They pushed her to the dining room where she was handed a hamburger. It was impossible for her to eat the sandwich, but she knew the gesture had been given in good fun and she was not embarrassed.

Rose Mary returned to Stillwater to find she had received orders to move to yet another base -- Dallas Naval Air Station.

But first, she was given two weeks leave.

At the train station in Terre Haute, Rose Mary's father looked pleased with her uniform and new smile. He insisted she have her photo taken.

Lulu Anderson had prepared a special Thanksgiving meal for her daughter. Time passed swiftly and soon, Rose Mary again stood at the train station, bags stuffed with wrapped Christmas gifts. She would wait to open them until the official holiday.

She rode a new streamline express train straight to Dallas where she caught a bus to the Naval Air Station, a small flight training school.

During the trip south, Rose Mary had developed a terrible cold. By the time she arrived at Naval Air Station, she felt terrible. When told her assignment was to work in the base library with what she discovered was an unfriendly civilian, Rose Mary felt worse.

She had joined the Navy to help the war effort. In her eyes, she had been doing more to help the war effort at the Ordinance Depot in Terre Haute.

On Christmas Day 1944, Rose Mary stood watch for a sailor so he could leave the base. On her first Christmas away from home, she spent it alone. When she tried to call her family, the phone lines were tied up.

Slowly, Rose Mary opened her suitcase and unwrapped the Christmas presents from her family. She dwelt on good memories from Thanksgiving. While she was not proud of her pity party, it was the best she could manage.

After Christmas, Rose Mary heard about a job opening in the security department of the base. The staff was in charge of security on the base and shore patrol. It sounded interesting and when a friend recommended her for the job, Rose Mary was grateful, doubly so when she was hired following an interview.

Rose Mary was put in charge of gas rationing on the base. She was sometimes confronted with unauthorized demands made to her by 'fliers' (pilots) who said they needed more gas than their allotted orders. Rose Mary stood firm.

Another time an officer tried to pull rank with his demand for extra gas. The base's legal officer overheard the conversation and set him straight.

Once a month, Rose Mary went to Dallas to make a deposit at a bank, always accompanied by a base security policeman.

The saddest part of her department's tasks was attending a dead service member's funeral. The department always supplied an honor guard of the same rank as the deceased.

It was not all work for Rose Mary and the other WAVES at Dallas. The base featured an indoor swimming pool, which the WAVES could use when it was available. Air crews also used it in teaching survival techniques. Wearing full flight gear, the trainees jumped from a catwalk into the pool and attempted to swim to safety.

At the war's end, Rose Mary Anderson was re-assigned to Camp Moffett at Naval Station Great Lakes in North Chicago, Illinois. She awaited a re-assignment to a base and maybe a discharge.

The latter would be welcome as she was now engaged. Throughout the war, Rose Mary and Richard had written letters. They had to wait for their discharges to find a date to be married.

On Christmas Day 1945, Richard called Rose Mary to say he had returned from the Pacific and was discharged. The war had not been kind to Richard. He had been severely burned when a make-shift stove exploded on him. But now he had healed and was in Chicago. He asked Rose Mary if she could get away to be married.

Rose Mary asked for and received a three-day pass. Lulu Anderson scrambled to make plans for her daughter's wedding. Rose Mary Anderson became Rose Mary Flener on February 16, 1946.

Two days later, after a brief honeymoon, Rose Mary caught a train back to Camp Moffett. There, she was discharged on March 7, 1946.

The Fleners became parents to three children. They lived in Fort Wayne where Rose Mary worked as a secretary and wrote family history.

Her thoughts: "If a woman wants to enter the military and can do everything the military asks of her, she should do it."

**

Words of the WAVES official song:

'There's a ship sailing down the bay, And she won't slip into port again until that vict'ry day. Carry on for that gallant ship and for every hero brave, Who will find ashore his man-sized chore was done by a Navy Wave.'

Rose Mary Anderson Flener joined the Navy to serve and to see the country.

Rosemary Russell Schmidt

Rosemary Russell had to make a decision.

In 1938, she had graduated from Quincy Senior High School in Quincy, Illinois. Rosemary loved reading and studying and hoped to go to college.

But the country continued to suffer from the Great Depression. Paying for college for most families was out of the question. Most people didn't have extra money for anything but essentials like food and clothing.

As the third oldest of six children, Rosemary didn't hold her breath that she would be able to further her education.

Rosemary's parents, Marguerite and Samuel Russell, had a plan. They wanted their children to make the most of their lives. They believed that could best be accomplished with college training.

Samuel Russell worked as a Director of Livestock for North Central College in Napierville, Illinois. Even though the cost of tuition for one student was $150.00, he worked hard to be able to send four of his children to college.

Rosemary enrolled at North Central College where she majored in biology. Upon graduating in 1942, she considered enrolling for pre-med courses.

Rosemary's mother had another idea.

The war had begun a few months earlier. The Navy needed female officers. "College graduates are automatic officers," she told Rosemary. "Maybe the Navy would be a good place for you."

Rosemary Russell took her mother's advice and applied to the WAVES program. She was accepted and enlisted in the Navy in early 1943.

The Russells would eventually have three members of the family in the war -- Rosemary's brother, Sam Jr., joined the Army; another brother, Keith, served in the Army Air Corps.

Rosemary was sent for three months of training to Smith College in Massachusetts. At the end of their time of learning Navy regulations, policies and practices, the WAVES officers were called '90 Day Wonders'.

Rosemary rode a train to Northampton, Massachusetts for more training. She was billeted in the Northampton Hotel with eight WAVES. Rosemary didn't mind sharing close quarters as she enjoyed meeting women from around the nation who were as focused as she on serving her country.

At Brooklyn Navy Yard in New York, Lieutenant Rosemary Russell was assigned as Communications Watch Officer. She and others in the communications (comm) department worked with coding and decoding messages sent between military installations around the world.

Each day the department received a new code which looked garbled. Code books in the office helped with translation. Messages received were assigned levels of priority depending on content, sender, and recipient. Messages with top priority received the most attention.

As the communications office was open 24/7, top priority messages could be received anytime. They needed to be delivered without haste.

Guards were on duty at the office building at all times.

Rosemary Russell and every other military personnel assigned to her department were given strict instructions about confidentiality. Never could they talk about their work to anyone. When Rosemary wrote to her parents, she filled her letters with information about what it was like to live in New York City.

Her parents expressed mixed emotions at her service. Samuel was proud of his daughter, while

Marguerite seemed concerned about Rosemary's safety in a big city.

Rosemary felt relatively safe living in a rented apartment which she shared with another WAVES. Each morning, they rode a commuter train to Grand Central Station where they then took the subway to Brooklyn Bridge and the Navy Yard.

In her spare moments Rosemary enjoyed the view from the windows of her office. Grand ships were being built in the shipyard for the war effort.

Rosemary once saw Margaret Truman christening the USS *Missouri*. Margaret was the daughter of Senator Harry Truman of Missouri who would later become President Franklin D. Roosevelt's running mate for his fourth term in 1944.

In 1944, Roosevelt would be re-elected, becoming the only United States president to be elected for four consecutive terms. At his death in April 1945, Truman was sworn in as president.

At the ship yard Rosemary Russell met First Lady Eleanor Roosevelt who asked what her military training had been like. Rosemary was inspired by both Margaret Truman and the First Lady and thought them charming.

Rosemary enjoyed her work, even though at the beginning of her service it required working holidays and weekends. As the number of WAVES increased, their work load was cut back to five days a week.

Rosemary found the work challenging and different than anything she had ever done. She reveled in it.

In general, the WAVES were treated with respect, although the Marine sentinel at the front gate of the base obviously regretted the necessity of saluting the women when they passed through.

Midway through the war, Rosemary Russell's personal life changed. While studying at North Central, she had met Robert Schmidt, a mechanical engineering student from Clarendon Hills, Illinois.

The couple had been engaged, but when war was declared, they held off making plans.

When Robert was drafted into the Navy, Rosemary hid her tears until his ship was out of sight. Then she let them flow while praying for his safety.

In March 1943, Robert called Rosemary. His ship had docked in Norfolk, Virginia. He only had a few days leave -- would she be willing to travel to Norfolk to get married?

She immediately asked for a few days leave which she was granted. They were married on March 24,

1943, by a Presbyterian minister in his home, witnessed by his wife.

A few days later, Robert left for another assignment in the South Pacific aboard a LST (landing, ship, tank).

During the next two years, Rosemary constantly prayed for her husband's safety. She was thrilled to receive an occasional letter from him on military stationery called V-mail ('victory mail). He could not tell her where he was and censors crossed out much of his information. Still, she was glad to know he was alive. She wrote him often, never knowing if her letters were received.

In September 1945, Japanese Imperial Forces surrendered. A month later, Rosemary was relieved of her command as Communication Watch Officer at the ship yard. When offered a promotion to Lieutenant Commander if she would re-enlist for five years, Rosemary turned down the offer. She was married and wanted to start a family.

After Robert's discharge in January 1946, they moved to Fort Wayne where he was hired as a mechanical engineer at International Harvester-Navistar. The couple became parents to three children.

Her thoughts: "Despite being separated from my husband for many months during the war, I enjoyed my work in the Navy. It was a unique experience. It was different than anything I had ever done and I tried hard to do a good job."

Rosemary Russell Schmidt served her country as an officer in the Navy, as well as the wife of a sailor.

Semper Paratus, Always Ready -- SPAR

Evelyn Ruth Beckman Brown

As the eldest child in her family, Evelyn Beckman felt a duty to serve her country during its time of war. 'Evie', as she was called by family, felt especially called upon to step up as she had three sisters and no brothers to send to fight.

The war that had dragged on for two years showed no signs of waning. The need to send more men overseas as replacements seemed unending. Evie wanted to help. But what could she do? No idea presented itself.

After graduating from Central High School in Fort Wayne, Indiana, in 1943, Evie found a job at a Social Security office.

Upon learning the armed forces were forming branches of service for women, Evie realized her opportunity of serving had presented itself. Each day, she haunted the Navy recruiting office near where she worked.

When the recruiter said the Navy had reached its quota for females, her hopes of serving in the military seemed dashed.

Then he said that the Coast Guard had openings for women. Evie didn't care which branch to join. She just wanted to serve.

The closest recruiting office for the Coast Guard was in Chicago, 150 miles from Fort Wayne.
In late January 1945, Evie and her mother, Pauline, rode a train to Chicago. Their plans were for Evie to enlist as a SPAR (this stood for the Coast Guard's motto in Latin, along with its translation: 'Semper Paratus, Always Ready.').

But when they reached the recruiting office, they learned a female had to be 21 years old or 20 years old with a parent's written permission. Evie was only 19 years old.

Dejected, Evie and her mother returned home. But they had not given up.

On February 28, they returned to the Windy City so Evie could be sworn in on her 20th birthday. Pauline Beckman provided written permission. A photo of Evie being sworn in appeared in a local newspaper.

Pauline Beckman's reaction to her daughter's desire to serve in the military might have surprised some.

During the Depression, Pauline Beckman had worked in a factory earning 19 cents an hour. She hoped her eldest daughter could experience the satisfaction of working at a respectable job while earning an acceptable wage.

Eight days later, Evelyn Beckman left on a train for boot camp with the Coast Guard Women's Reserve at Manhattan Beach.

Evie learned to march, take orders, perform drills, and help in the dining hall after meals. Later, at Yeoman School she perfected skills from high school in shorthand and typing.

She enjoyed it all and thought she had died and gone to heaven when receiving an assignment at the lovely Coast Guard Academy in New London, Connecticut.

Evie marveled at the beautiful campus. Though nervous at first, she quickly grew accustomed to her duties and resolved to do her best in her responsibilities as a secretary to an officer.

Many forms that came across her desk were for military leaves and discharges as it was now May 1945 and the war was over in Europe.

Barracks for the SPARS were not established so the women found housing using Coast Guard stipends for subsistence and quarters (S&Q). Evie roomed with SPARs from New Jersey, Iowa, and Brooklyn.

After the war, she would keep in contact with many of these women for decades.

Dress code for SPARs included uniform dresses and blue slacks. The women were only allowed to wear the pants when it was the Uniform of the Day or doing KP duty. Those were the first pants Evie Beckman had ever worn.

As the SPARs were required to keep hair off of their collars, Evie wore hers short. They were also not allowed to wear jewelry.

With her meals, clothing, and housing provided, Evie had her needs met. Knowing her family, like many across the nation, was restricted with food items like sugar and meat, she sent part of her paychecks home for her family's use.

While Evie Beckman might have felt sorry for her family, she was not homesick. She kept in touch through letters. But her family knew that being in the Coast Guard was an adventure for her.

When off-duty, Evie Beckman frequented a service center for the Coast Guard set up with snacks, music, and games. Naval and submarine bases in the area hosted social times that the women could attend.

Male Coast Guardsmen trained as officers at the academy but had little contact with the women, eating in a separate mess (dining) hall.

During leaves, Evie and the SPARs toured New York City. They visited the Empire State Building, Statue of Liberty, Rockefeller Center, Radio City Music Hall, and Waldorf Astoria.

When the war ended in September 1945 with the Japanese surrender, Evie would have re-enlisted, if given the chance like the male Coast Guardsmen.

Instead, she was prepared mentally for June 20, 1946, as the final day of the SPAR program. Evie resolved to remain at her post as long as possible to help with the transition.

As it happened, Evie was the last SPAR at the academy on the date of closure. She typed her own discharge papers. She had served 15 months and 12 days.

Back in Fort Wayne, Evie found a job as a teller at Anthony Wayne Bank. She married Ronald Vernon Brown and they became parents to four children.

Evie completed nurses training and worked for 28 years at Aiken Clinic in Fort Wayne. In 2011 she participated in Honor Flight of Northeast Indiana.

For many years she was part of veteran parades and events.

Her thoughts:

"I was never a hero. As a SPAR, I did a job I was capable of doing to take the place of an able-bodied male who could fight the real battle. I hope my story will reflect my desire to serve my country, my pleasure in meeting and working with others, my appreciation of places I was able to see and my patriotic pride in serving as a SPAR."

Evelyn Beckman Brown worked at the Coast Guard Academy until the SPAR program closed on July 20, 1946. She typed her own discharge papers.

Lorraine Hook Davis

During World War II, Lorraine Hook's work was top-secret. Nothing she did each day could be shared with anyone, including family.

Lorraine was born in 1920 in Aliquippa, Pennsylvania. Upon graduating from New Castle High School in 1937, she attended Muskingum University (then called Muskingum College) in New Concord, Ohio. World War II Navy pilot and future astronaut John Glenn was a classmate.

As the country was still in the throes of the Great Depression, Lorraine, who had been brought up to be industrious, paid for her tuition by working as a secretary.

After graduating in 1941 with a degree in business, Lorraine worked two years at General Electric Lighting in Nela Park, Ohio.

When the Japanese attacked Pearl Harbor on December 7, 1941, Lorraine's life, like that of millions of people around the world, changed. As the country geared up for war, she watched as thousands of young men – many of whom she had gone to school with – were drafted for military service.

Lorraine felt useless in her job, especially as on March 17, 1942, the government announced that coal, gas, and electricity were to be rationed. She wanted to be part of what was happening with her generation. She believed that, although women were not allowed in combat, she could contribute to the war effort in the military.

That fall in Cleveland, Ohio, Lorraine Hook took the Navy officer test as part of the WAVES recruitment. The application included physical and written exams for college graduates who had two years of work experience.

A female friend accompanied her and also took the tests. When the pair was told the Coast Guard was recruiting women, they decided to apply there as well. Lorraine and her friend believed since the Coast Guard was a smaller branch, they'd be more likely to serve together.

The good news was that both women were accepted in the Coast Guard. But they were immediately separated and sent to different assignments.

In March 1943, Lorraine was ordered to Gillett Hall at Smith College in Massachusetts for training in communication, specifically cryptography. First Lieutenant Hook received preliminary training for a few weeks before being sent to Northampton Hotel in Northampton, Massachusetts for more education in communications.

She and other SPARs trained with plain language and code, memorized facts and figures, and devised systems for remembering vital information for tests at the training station.

The SPARs marched to classes, dormitories and their chow hall at the Hotel Northampton. They also spent two hours a day doing physical education exercises and drills to stay physically fit.

With all of the energy expended for drills, Lorraine and the other SPARs were delighted with the food at the Northampton Hotel which they considered almost gourmet.

The SPAR officers paid for their uniforms like male officers. Each woman was responsible for cleaning and pressing her uniforms. The women's dresses were similar to that of the WAVES, except for the buttons and insignia of the Coast Guard. They wore their rank on their collars.

In March 1943, a special event occurred for the SPARs in Northampton when Eleanor Roosevelt visited.

She was tall and not particularly prepossessing until she got up to speak. Then the First Lady entranced her audience, including Lorraine. It was a life-changing experience for the young officer.

On Sundays Lorraine attended services at the Episcopal Church and joined other SPARs in singing the navy hymn. Occasionally, she went to a theater and particularly enjoyed the 1942 film, 'Casablanca.'

Lorraine Hook sometimes entertained male visitors in the SPAR dayroom. But for the most part, she and the other women led quiet lives, glad to relax when off-duty.

After six weeks, Lorraine was sent to the Coast Guard Academy in New London, Connecticut, where she was billeted with other SPARs in Hamilton Hall.

The Men's Coast Guard Reserves were on the same campus. Although the SPARs had no contact, each morning Lorraine could hear the men chanting as they carried heavy lifeboats to a lake to row before breakfast.

Upon graduating from SPAR training, Lorraine was sent to Washington DC for orientation for Coast Guard procedures. After a few weeks, she was again transferred – this time to Boston where the Communications Department operated in three floors of the old Customs House near the harbor.

The building, which was heavily guarded by armed military personnel, contained a code room where Lorraine worked in the basement. Machines included teletypes on which 16 enlisted SPARS worked.

The code room was connected to the radio station. Five SPAR comm officers were assigned to the radios, while two SPARs served as messengers.

Strict procedures applied to their work. Allied military officials transmitted new codes daily. No names were attached to messages. Lorraine's department contained reference books with keys to codes used at American military installations around the world.

At one point Lorraine was made supervising officer for the comm center. She was tasked with reading each message before deciding if it should be sent on to bases throughout the United States and Hawaii. If something didn't read right, she questioned the typist.

At the beginning of the war, the need for cryptographers was so great that the SPARs worked 24 hours a day, seven days a week. As more women were trained, the work load was reduced to five days.

The arrival of SPARs allowed men who had been performing cryptography jobs to be assigned to ships. Lorraine never encountered direct resentment by the men at the harbor. Most seemed to accept the SPARs as helpful and efficient.

From windows overlooking Boston Harbor the SPARs could observe ships that arrived through the harbor entrance control post. Movements of every ship were recorded.

One of the most spectacular sites for Lorraine was seeing ice-covered ships arrive from Greenland, a country the Allies patrolled. She knew that while their sparkling appearance may have dazzled her, it was not so beatific for the men on board who were probably freezing!

After work hours, Lorraine and other WAVES frequented the officer's club where they danced with male Coast Guardsmen. Other times Lorraine attended concerts of the Boston Pops Orchestra.

With her busy life Lorraine didn't feel homesick. She had already lived and worked on her own after college. In the Coast Guard she felt efficient and independent.

In July 1945, Lorraine received a new assignment. The war in Europe had ended, but the Allies planned a major invasion in Japan. She was sent to Honolulu to help prepare for this massive undertaking.

Lorraine worked with the comm officers assigned in Honolulu's code room. She also worked as duty officer during night shifts.

In her free time, she visited Honolulu. After three and a half years of war, it was without doubt a sailor's town. Tourism had virtually halted so the city only featured three hotels. When her schedule permitted, Lorraine attended an Episcopal Church and the base chapel.

On August 15, 1945, news arrived that Japan had surrendered. Lorraine didn't have duty that night, but she was at Bachelor Officer Quarters (BOQ). She and the other Coast Guardsmen watched from windows of the second floor as jubilant crowds in the city created a cacophony of noise about the war's end and the Allied victory.

As ships in the harbor shot off rockets in celebration, Lorraine was reminded of Francis Scott Key's lyrics in the 'Star-Spangled Banner': "and the rockets' red glare, the bombs bursting in air."

Lorraine remained in Hawaii until February 1946. Her work was different from when she had arrived. All over the world, American troops were being sent home. She had little to do.

Truth was, though anxious to see her family, Lorraine Hook hated to leave the SPARs. She had no choice of re-enlisting as on June 30, 1946, the SPAR program ended.

Lorraine left Hawaii, knowing she had had a unique opportunity to work with intelligent men and women whom she would always consider friends.

She did have something to look forward to. In Hawaii, she had met a man whom she had fallen in love with. He had already returned to the States and she planned to meet him to discuss their future together.

Then, days before leaving the islands, Lorraine received devastating news -- her fiancé had been killed in a motor vehicle accident.

By the time she arrived in the States, Lorraine's thoughts were in shreds. Everything she had planned for her life was gone.

Slowly, Lorraine took stock of her life. She had always enjoyed learning. She used the GI Bill, which had been established for military personnel to have access to benefits like a college education, to enroll at Purdue University. She would earn a Master's degree in education.

At Purdue Lorraine Hook met Miles Davis, a pharmaceutical student, also attending on the GI Bill. He had fought at Utah Beach during D-Day.

Lorraine and Miles fell in love and married. Miles accepted a job with a pharmacy in Huntington, Indiana. When Miles was recalled for military service during the Korean War, Lorraine experienced life, not as a military person, but as a military spouse.

After Miles returned from Korea, the Davises moved to Fort Wayne where they became parents to two sons. Lorraine taught English at Central High School, while Miles set up a pharmacy.

Her thoughts: "I really enjoyed my military service. My job in Communications in the Coast Guard suited me. I still feel a great loyalty to my country and the Coast Guard."

Lorraine Hook Davis served in the United States and Hawaii before being discharged from the Coast Guard.

History of Women at War

Women have been part of the American military since the inception of the United States. The American Revolution was a success due to the contributions of women like Deborah Sampson, Margaret Corbin, and Mary Ludwig Hays.

During the American Civil War, an estimated 600 to 1,000 women disguised themselves as men to enlist in both the union and confederate armies.

Also during the Civil War, nursing became a more legitimized profession with over 21,000 women providing care in union military hospitals.

At the turn of the 20th century, women's participation in the military became more legitimized, with the creation of the Army Nurse Corps and Navy Nurse Corps, in 1901 and 1908, respectively.

World War I afforded more opportunities for women to serve in the armed forces, from the "yeomanettes" to the Marine Corps Women's Reserve. However after the war, these women were denied the same benefits as their male counterparts and the women's reserves were ended.

In May of 1941, Congresswoman Edith Nourse Rogers introduced a bill to create a Women's Army

Auxiliary Corps (WAAC). Passage of the bill occurred on May 14, 1942 and the first women to enlist in the Army began training in July 1942.

That year, other branches of the US military followed suit with the Navy's WAVES, the Marine Corps' Women's Reserve, and the Coast Guard's SPARS.

In July 1943 the WAAC dropped its auxiliary status and became the Women's Army Corps (WAC)— the first time women had actual military status in the US Army. The Army Nurse Corps would drop their relative rank system and gain full status in 1944.

Women of the WAVES, USMCWR, and SPARS served in the states and Hawaii in vital support roles throughout the war. Army women served stateside and overseas in every theater of war.

Members of the WASP (Women Airforce Service Pilots) had the highest casualty rate of any of the uniformed services, but never gained military status.

-- Molly Sampson, Historian & Museum Professional

Book Discussion Questions

1. Several women in the book encountered opposition to their decisions to join the military. When has someone voiced negativity to a decision you made – new career, marital partner, location? How did you handle it?

2. Betty Dybbro left home without telling her family she was joining the WASP. What would you feel if someone in your family left in a similar way?

3. Have you known a female in the military? What did you think of her decision? If you are a female who joined the military, what made you decide to enlist?

4. Which woman in the book did you identify with and why?

5. Imagine you are a 21-year-old female in 1943. Would you join the military, work in a factory, or other for the war effort? Explain.

6. Bonnie Habegger and Eileen Zeissig prayed about going to Japan during the invasion. What approach do you take when faced with difficult life situations?

7. Despite being forced out of the Coast Guard, Evelyn Brown supported the military throughout her life. Give an example of when

you showed loyalty to a group or organization.

8. Polly Woodhull and other nurses had to refrain from dating enlisted men. What do you think of the rules against fraternization? Should the military continue to enforce these rules?

9. Marty Wyall's father insisted she finish college before enlisting in the WASP. The delay caused her to be in the last class. What do you think of his insistence that she graduate?

10. What incident from the book impressed you the most? Explain.

Read an excerpt from *It Was Our War Too: Youth in the Shadows of WWII*, based on an interview the author conducted with a British member of the *Women's Royal Naval Service (WRN)*

Marigold 'Margot' Wilson McNeely

Marigold 'Margot' Wilson was 13 years old when war between England and Germany broke out in 1939. Born in London, she lived with her family at Burnham-on-Sea in southwestern England.

In May 1940, Hitler, having already taken over most of Europe, ordered his German Air Force (Luftwaffe) to drop bombs on London and other British cities in an attempt to force Great Britain to surrender.

Although some people believed living in the English countryside during the war was safer than in London, Margot knew otherwise. "Dogfights occurred between English Spitfires and German fighters over our homes," she said. "Shrapnel fell on the roofs."

Margot attended La Retraite Sacred Heart Convent in Somerset. When air-raid alerts sounded, students and staff ran to underground shelters and cellars.

"We carried gas masks with us at all times," she said. Fortunately, she never had to use it.

The gas masks provided humor for the students. "It was a challenge not to laugh at the nuns in their black habits teaching while wearing their masks," said Margot.

After graduating from the convent at age 17, Margot volunteered to join the Women's Royal Naval Service (WRNs).

At age 18 English boys and girls were conscripted into service for their country. They could be assigned to the military, factories or farms. "As I had grown up near the seaside, I wanted to be in the Navy," said Margot. Her mother gave her blessing on the choice.

Margot was sent to work at Bletchley Park. The top-secret post an hour north of London was where decoding of enemy messages occurred. Famed mathematician and logician Alan Turing worked on the computer called the Bombe which broke the Nazi Enigma code.

Margot was also assigned to Eastcote, 30 minutes from London on the Underground (tube train). "We worked eight-hour shifts around the clock for a week or ten days before getting leave time," she said.

Kayleen Reusser Books

World War II Legacies:

We Fought to Win: American WWII Veterans Share Their Stories (Book 1)

They Did It for Honor: Stories of American WWII Veterans (Book 2)

We Gave Our Best: American WWII Veterans Tell Their Stories (Book 3)

We Defended Freedom: Adventures of WWII Veterans (Book 4)

World War II Insider:

D-Day: Soldiers, Sailors and Airmen Tell about Normandy (Book 1)

Battle of the Bulge: Stories From Those Who Fought and Survived (Book 2)

Captured! Stories of American WWII Prisoners of War (Book 1, Prisoners of War)

It Was Our War Too: Youth in the Shadows of WWII (Book 1, Witnesses of War)

Women of WWII Coloring Book

About the Author

Kayleen Reusser has written about hundreds of World War II veterans. Her books are available on Amazon.

Subscribe to her Youtube Channel to hear short talks by veterans she has interviewed talk about their service.

As a speaker (virtual and in-person), Reusser presents talks about World War II-related topics. For contact information and to sign up for her newsletter and blog go to KayleenReusser.com.

www.ingramcontent.com/pod-product-compliance
Lightning Source LLC
Chambersburg PA
CBHW060323050426
42449CB00011B/2629